AMERICAN POETS PROJECT

AMERICAN POETS PROJECT

IS PUBLISHED WITH A GIFT IN MEMORY OF

James Merrill

AND SUPPORT FROM ITS FOUNDING PATRONS

Sidney J. Weinberg, Jr. Foundation

The Berkley Foundation

Richard B. Fisher and Jeanne Donovan Fisher

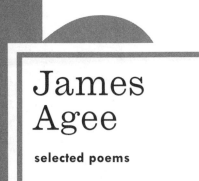

James Agee

selected poems

andrew hudgins editor

AMERICAN POETS PROJECT

THE LIBRARY OF AMERICA

Design by Chip Kidd and Mark Melnick.
Frontispiece: Copyright © Helen Levitt, Courtesy Laurence Miller Gallery, New York. All rights reserved.

Library of Congress Control Number: 2008929054
ISBN 978-1-59853-032-2
American Poets Project—27

10 9 8 7 6 5 4 3 2 1

James
Agee

CONTENTS

INTRODUCTION

In a brief introduction to *Permit Me Voyage* (1934), James Agee's first book and the only volume of his poetry published during his lifetime, Archibald MacLeish notes wryly that Agee "has a considerable contempt for the dying civilization in which he has spent twenty-four years." But along with his "deep love of the land," Agee according to MacLeish came by the contempt through hard experience, having "spent his boyhood, with his fair share of the disadvantages so generously bestowed by the not-quite-existing order, in and about the Cumberland Mountains, and some of his vacation time during his Harvard years he spent as a harvest stiff in the Kansas and Nebraska wheat fields."

MacLeish was right as far as he went, but unfairly dismissive to imply, however lightly, that Agee's rage grew from a young man's callowness. Even at 24, Agee was already a well-read Romantic who came of age at the beginning of the Great Depression. His youthful sense of justice *was* aggrieved to the point of revulsion by America's social and economic inequities, but he was also, at the time he wrote *Permit Me Voyage*, a lifelong Christian deeply immersed in Platonism by way of St. Paul. His contempt for the world was not just a young man's balked idealism but also the intellectual response of a believer steeped in the major texts of his faith. The author of the sonnet "So it begins. Adam is in his earth"—the first poem in an impressive sequence of 25 sonnets in *Permit Me Voyage*—is clearly acquainted with Karl Marx, and he has read Herbert, Donne, and Hopkins closely. But the poem is utterly American; it speaks in the voice of an educated American who had been immersed for two decades in the King James Bible and The Book of Common Prayer. Agee was an instinctive believer who had done his homework, and his judgment of Western Civilization paralleled T. S. Eliot's, but from the political left.

"So it begins. Adam is in his earth" makes a useful point of entry into Agee's poetry. The stated worldview is about as bleak as anything that John Calvin ever formulated, but the poem crackles with the poet's love for the precision and ironic felicity that he brings to bear in expressing the human predicament. The restrained rhythms of the sonnet's opening suggests a preacher's theatrical delight in grasping the sides of the pulpit and making a deceptively soothing statement—"So it begins. Adam is in his earth"—before accelerating harshly to "Tempted, and fallen, and his doom made sure." Paradise is offered and then snatched away.

In Agee's case, the preacher in the back of his mind might conceivably be one of the conservative Anglo-Catholic priests he heard throughout his childhood and adolescence. After the death of his father, his mother had become more and more religious, even insisting that James, who was six when his father died, be circumcised. When Agee was 14, his mother remarried and James became the stepson of a priest. He was a thoroughly churched boy, one who must have known in his bones how to structure a sermon, and, in the manner of a sermon, the pitch of the sonnet rises through the octet, as the bitter innate *hungers* and *ravenings* that afflicted Adam from even before his birth culminate, we are told, only at his death.

At the first word of the ninth line—"Meantime he works the earth, and builds up nations"—the poem pauses. What can be worse, now that Adam is released from his desires by death? Is the poem, like a sermon, going to move from present misery to the hope for salvation? After the deep breath of that "meantime," the poem takes a step backward—Adam is still alive—and forward at the same time, through the generations. History works itself out as theological fate. Following his *hungerings*, which are both Christian sins and Marxist transgressions, Adam builds the civilization that Ezra Pound had already described as "an old bitch gone in the teeth" and that Agee himself in a late poem about America at the end of World War II would call with even greater savagery "A dying grandmother, babbling of a ball: / Take her just so, Death; let her enjoy it all." By a deft bit of rhetorical legerdemain in the sonnet's sestet, the first father of Genesis becomes each of us, and he, who is also we, creates the trading, warring, and worshipping of chance that will persist beyond our deaths through the generations after us. We Adams also have an inclination toward learning and an impulse to look toward God, though those hopeful endeavors are squeezed in between the treacherous pursuits we clearly favor.

When the poem arrives at its end, which is also an inversion of its beginning, the tone is despairing, but the poet is no longer passing judgment on others so much as on himself. Given that Adam is everyone, the logic of the poem narrows ineluctably down to a particular one, the poet himself. The public has become personal and the poet accepts, because he has to, the burden of history, human nature, and the Christian mythos as his own.

*

James Agee's early achievements as a poet, of which this sonnet sequence is a notable instance, have been over-shadowed by his prose, though the adjective most often mobilized to describe the prose is "poetic." What is he best known for? For many his masterpiece is *Let Us Now Praise Famous Men* (1941), a precursor to the New Journalism, with its wrenchingly self-conscious reporting of Agee's two months living with a family of grindingly poor sharecroppers in Hale County, Alabama. Film buffs would insist on the importance of his early and seminal film reviews in *Time* and *The Nation*, as well as his screenplays for *The African Queen* (1954) and *The Night of the Hunter* (1955). Lovers of prose fiction, though, could make a more than reasonable claim for the priority of his lovely novella *The Morning Watch* (1951) and the poignant autobiographical novel *A Death in the Family*, published posthumously in 1957, which received the Pulitzer Prize.

And many readers will stand up for the priority of Agee as an epistolary stylist based on his letters to his friend Father Flye, who had been his teacher at St. Andrew's School in Sewanee, Tennessee. These rich letters, published in 1971, give us the full figure of a boy and man who loved literature and wrote about it with great warmth. Here, for instance, is Agee's precocious yet cogent assessment of Dreiser's *An American Tragedy*, written on April 20, 1927, when he was a 17-year-old student at Phillips Exeter: "Dreiser's English is bum, yet it has a peculiar beauty and excellence. You feel you are reading a rather inadequate translation of a very great foreign novel—Russian probably. He's horribly obvious, and has no humor. But this dullness is a relief from the heady brilliance of Dos Passos or Lewis—and he has a tenderness, a love for his characters, that rarely slobbers and is usually strong and fine." A reader can hear the loving critic's desire to be precise in both his criticism and his praise, as well the pride of the young man—boy, really—flexing his intelligence and sensibility in the act of forming that sensibility. But first, last, and at every step in between, James Agee was not just a writer of poetic prose, but a poet too. It's true that the impulse to poetry was strongest when Agee was young, something the poet himself realized as early as 23, when he wrote Father Flye:

> One thing I feel is this: that a great deal of poetry is the product of adolescence—or of an emotionally adolescent frame of mind: and that as this state of mind changes, poetry is likely to dry up. I think most people let it; and that the one chance is to keep fighting and trying as hard as possible. That doesn't hold water—nothing I think does now. But it seems somewhat better to try than to quit the job entirely.

Less than a year later, Archibald MacLeish, Agee's superior at *Fortune*, gave Agee's manuscript of poems to Stephen Vincent Benét, the editor of the Yale Younger Poets series. Benét selected Agee's submission from the 42 he had on hand, and *Permit Me Voyage* was published to tepid reviews. Agee never again worked on his poetry with such concentrated energy, although he did continue to write it and write it well. After Agee's death, the poet and translator Robert Fitzgerald, a close friend, edited *The Collected Poems of James Agee* (1962), giving us most but not all of the poems written after *Permit Me Voyage*. (The present volume contains nearly all of what Fitzgerald gathered, although with a shorter sample of the unfinished epic "John Carter," while adding several poems not in *The Collected Poems*.)

Agee was as restless in his poetry as he was later in his prose. His poetry has the variety we might expect from the protean mind that excelled in so many different kinds of writing. He is after all the man who, in a 1937 application for a Guggenheim fellowship, listed 47 projects he wanted to pursue. The same enthusiasm informed Agee's openly declared love for his influences. The first lyric of *Permit Me Voyage* echoes Housman and Auden, as well as Marvell, Donne, and who knows what other poets, though with an unnerving ironic ferocity that reaches beyond its influences.

> Child, should any pleasant boy
> Find you lovely, many could,
> Wind not up between your joy
> The sly delays of maidenhood:
>
> Spread all your beauty in his sight
> And do him kindness every way,
> Since soon, too soon, the wolfer night
> Climbs in between, and ends fair play.

The rakish eyebrow arched over "many could" and the predatory, punning "wolfer" are all Agee. From the beginning, as throughout Agee's work, Eros and Thanatos are inseparable.

In the radically different "Dedication," a prose poem, Agee melds touches of Walt Whitman and The Book of Common Prayer. After a devotional prayer ("in much humility / to God in the highest / in the trust that he despises nothing), he goes on to dedicate the poem, the book, and his life to everyone from, first, Christ, and then to Dante, Beethoven, Swift, "the fathers of the Holy Scripture," to "an unknown sculpture of China, for his god's head," before turning to his family and friends, and back to God again. With an irony reminiscent of Villon's *Testament* he also dedicates the book to the "those merchants, dealers and speculators" who should examine curiously, and honestly into their own hearts, and see how surely and to what extent they in themselves are blood-guilty; and how and in what manifold ways they are more subtly and terribly and vastly accountable than for life blood alone: and that they repent their very existence of the men they are, and change or quit it: or visit the just curse upon themselves.

In its commodiousness and high oracular voice the poem adumbrates Agee's later prose style.

The leap from the charged prose of "Dedication" to "Ann Garner," a long narrative poem written when Agee was still at prep school, is startling. Evoking Robert Frost's "Home Burial," the poem begins with the birth and burial of Ann and her husband's stillborn child "in the frozen earth." But when Ann becomes a fertility figure to her neighbors ("As long as Ann lived, all the countryside / Was rich in produce—as long as Ann lived"), the poem somewhat clumsily but with real power picks up a mythic expansiveness derived from Robinson Jeffers.

It is even more surprising to move from "Ann Garner" to tight and dense metaphysical poems like "A Chorale" and "Epithalamium," and "Permit Me Voyage," which ends the book. Probably the best known of Agee's poems, "Permit Me Voyage" takes its title and final line from the third section of Hart Crane's "Voyages," in which Crane celebrates his physical love for Emil Opffer. Agee's poem is both an answer to and a tip of the hat to Crane. Agee isn't so much correcting Crane, though, as extending his erotic vision to include the source of Eros, God, and to subsume Eros in *agape*. In Agee's hands, Crane's plea to his love becomes a prayer, and the "love" of Crane's poem becomes "Love" with a capital L, directly addressed to God.

> I know
> How labors with Godhead this day:
>
> How from the porches of our sky
> The crested glory is declined:
> And hear with what translated cry
> The stridden soul is overshined:
>
> And how this world of wildness through
> True poets shall walk who herald you:
> Of whom God grant me of your grace
> To be, that shall preserve this race.

Both Crane and Agee saw their poetry as hopeful alternatives to the despairing Eliot, though in different ways. For Agee, the Christian poet, through his prayerful art, can rescue, or at least preserve, what Pound called a "botched civilization."

Agee stated his goal of bringing together faith, art, and social transformation even more explicitly in his application for a Guggenheim fellowship. With "John Carter," a poem "somewhat after the manner of *Don Juan*," Agee hoped to create "a widespread popular awareness of the prevailing validity of religious faith and of religious and artistic morality as opposed to 'scientific mortality'" and "to help change (if it can be changed) the prevalent negative state of mind into a positive state." That's a lot to ask of a poem, and as Agee's sense of his faith waned so did the impulse behind the poem. More sustaining was his desire, proclaimed in the same application, "to use the American Language as a sort of cement for all other dictions: to make it valid in all kinds of poetry." And it's clear from a passage from "John Carter" that he read the American poets of his time with a weather eye, assessing Edwin Arlington Robinson ("One Neo-Arthurian scales the dread subjunctive /

Gathering samphire with a neat desk-knife"), Robert Frost ("One farmer's verse in splendor might be dunked, if / His hired man, farmer, or the farmer's wife / Shut up their dismal dialectic squawking / For even five lines, and let *him* do the talking"), Robinson Jeffers ("One Californian's vision is gigantic / In images alone; his line's too long"), and T. S. Eliot ("One of great but singular ability, / Contrived expert symbolic bellyaches, / Toiled thence to higher, drier debility").

"John Carter" has been unjustly maligned as the poem that stalled Agee as a serious poet. Yes, it fails in its aim to emulate Byron, and the narrative on which Agee hoped to hang his digressions was clearly misconceived: "It's to be the life-story of one John Carter, who humanly speaking is the typical American Young Man: spiritually speaking, he is an orthodox Roman Catholic devil, God-given to the world, a New Messiah of Evil." Agee quickly loses interest in the story—at about stanza ten by my reckoning—because his true impulses are lyric first and satirical second, but "John Carter"—of which the first and most achieved section is presented here—still has wonderful riffs that would make fine poems on their own.

Agee's range also encompasses strong free verse, a form he did not use very often, perhaps because his free verse was close in texture and subject to his prose. But when he did, the poetry was powerful and moving. In "Sunday: Outskirts of Knoxville, Tennessee," the couple's innocent, dreamlike, and Romantic oneness with nature is short-lived. Almost immediately their love, like everything else, is subject to convention, clashing desires, and the debilitations of time. The clear eye of the poet, though, is not cold, and as often with Agee the poem ends with a conflicted prayer. God is beseeched to show the young couple the future so they can avoid it, a supplication immediately followed by the horrifying but even more compassionate plea that they be blinded so they will not see the unavoidable playing out of their love. Agee's wit engages some of the mortifications the couple will suffer. In this list of escalating humiliations, the last would have troubled the antibourgeois poet more than the first two: "Policies, incapacities, a chevrolet."

In the variety of his work, and then the variety inside each genre, we can't help seeing what looks like a commitment to the dazzlingly fragmentary. Agee's early fixation on death—a tendency to which his growing alcoholism could only have contributed—led him almost inevitably to appreciate the virtues of failure. The poems derive their energy from their own internal conflicts in trying to become American and to absorb their many influences; the journalism of *Let Us Now Praise Famous Men*, a failure in its own time, remains heavy with a self-absorption that approaches hysteria; the movie criticism never quite becomes a coherent whole; the screenplays, although brilliant, were produced only in part or not at all; the great novel is piercing, beautiful, and perhaps great, but was not actually completed; the superb letters for all their honesty and self-criticism don't quite attain a transforming self-understanding. Yet Agee delivers in huge measure the pleasures—eminently Romantic—of the glittering fragment.

As a young writer for *Fortune*, Agee brought his record player to work and at night cranked it up full blast as he smoked, drank, and wrote in the empty offices on the 50th floor of the Chrysler Building. The best way to listen to music, he tells us in the introduction of *Let Us Now Praise Famous Men*, is to absorb it through the body:

Get a radio or a phonograph capable of the most extreme loudness possible, and sit down to listen to a performance of Beethoven's Seventh Sympathy or of Schubert's C-Major Symphony. But I don't mean just sit down and listen. I mean this: Turn it on as loud as you can get it. Then get down onto the floor and jam your ear as close into the loudspeaker as you can get it and stay there, breathing as lightly as possible, and not moving, and neither eating nor smoking nor drinking. Concentrate everything you can into your hearing and into your body. You won't hear it nicely. If it hurts you, be glad of it. As near as you will ever get, you are inside the magic; not only inside it, you are it; your body is no longer your shape and substance, it is the shape and substance of the music.

Is what you hear pretty? or beautiful? or legal? or acceptable in polite or any other society? It is beyond any calculation savage and dangerous and murderous to all equilibrium in human life as human life is; and nothing can equal the rape it does on all that death; nothing except anything, anything in existence or dream, perceived anywhere remotely toward its true dimension.

Perhaps he is also telling us how to listen to writing, especially his own writing.

Despite the Dionysian trappings—the three marriages and numerous affairs, the breakneck smoking and drinking that killed him at 45—James Agee was a Calvinist at the bone and a moralist at the marrow. When Agee later departed from the hard Anglo-Catholic faith of his childhood, the God-hunger persisted and the moral imperative grew more generalized. But from the beginning he saw himself as a truth-teller who valued instinct over logic. In an undergraduate poem ("All seasons pass, once more they swerve above") he inveighed against poets who "flaw truth with beauty." But his moralism and truth-telling do not

lead to the kind of stiff and sniffy writing we might antici-
pate. When he sees people and not corporations, raw com-
passion is held in check only by the judging eye.

Consider the song, one of "Three Cabaret Songs,"
that begins:

> Wake up Threeish,
>   Clean up the sink
> Air out the bedroom
>   Pour out a drink
> Drink to the daylight
>   Sit down and think
> I'm Open All Night.

The coarse sexual pun on "open all night" gathers, with
repetition, a louche charm appropriate for a cabaret song.
The poem's criticism is not of the young woman speaker or
her sexuality but of a society that has stranded her between
a traditional woman's role as wife and mother and a "freer"
role that is not yet clear. In 1932 he had written to Father
Flye about women of his time in transition from "trying to
live an uneasy egocentricity they can't sustain, unable to
reconcile it with love, which they could, and ruined in love
by the grinding of old conventions to which they've been
trained, against new conventions which they honestly feel
compelled to live by . . ."

Agee's song is broader in tone and narrower in vision
than the section in Eliot's "The Waste Land" in which the
"young man carbuncular" "makes a welcome" of the typ-
ist's sexual indifference. If Agee's flapped-out flapper lacks
the intellectual weight of Eliot's numb typist, neither is she
burdened with Eliot's corrosive repugnance for sex and
the two shallow people who in his poem engage in it. Agee,
the famous night owl and profligate, disapproves of his
young woman's feckless life because she isn't enjoying it,

and he appreciates her dilemma. He too has been open all night. In her voice, he empathizes with the Adam of either sex who is "sunken dead among his sins" as he phrases it in "So it begins. Adam is in his earth."

The weight of original sin—the theme of the 25-sonnet sequence—does not encompass the whole of Agee's vision, even if it represents an inevitable starting point. By 1935, he would attempt, in the unpublished poem "Him we killed and laid alone," to resolve the problem with a stab at dualism that seems to borrow both its rhythm and Manichaeism from Blake. Christ looks at those "for whose love his life was paid" and grants "each a cloven hand / Forth from the ruined realm of shade / Before God's light as I believe / Leads out Adam, leads out Eve." Another poem from 1935 moves past even heresy to an explicit re-nunciation of faith: in "When Eve first saw the glittering day," Eve lies down and cries. Adam, as undeterred by her grief as the "young man carbuncular" is by the typist's lack of interest, "climbed his bride with all his might / And sank to gentlest rest."

But Agee's poetry is strongest when he still grips, how-ever frantically, his faith. The struggle to comprehend his place in God's vision is a bulwark against creeping doubt, and the restraints of poetic form become a bulwark against the excesses and narcissism that mar his greater work in prose. By sonnet XX of the sequence—"Now stands our love on that still verge of day"—Agee has worked his way to a new and longed-for vision: "So stands our love new found and unaroused, / Appareled in all peace and inno-cence." He lingers in this entrancing state until the first sentence of the next sonnet, which dismisses the delusion with Swiftean nausea as "One swill of dreams that all ways wreak him spite."

After turning his back on his false vision of reclaimed

innocence, Agee tries to find a truer understanding of his relationship to God. He eschews what sonnet XXII calls "the noise of logic," which leads people into ideologies, greed, and self-advancement, and returns to looking honestly into his own heart, or as sonnet XXIII says, "Such songs I shall not make nor truths shall know: / And once more mindless into truth shall go." That reverential and instinctive mindlessness also means stepping beyond his literary influences: "Those immense souls who have peopled mine too long" (sonnet XXIV). In the final sonnet, he states, with colloquial American directness: "This mouth that blabbed so loud with foreign song / I'll shut awhile, or gargle if I sing."

Sonnet XXV is a prayer, and the poem and the sequence as a whole close with a direct pledge to God, even if Agee knows he will fail in his devotion. He will reject the intellectual search for truth, which leads to blindness or hate, but his heart cannot be entirely counted on either. It is "cloven," like Satan's goat foot, and whether Agee's impulses are godly or demonic is hidden from him. But when he makes the wrong choice, he knows whom to blame:

> These are confusing times and dazed with fate:
> Fear, easy faith, or wrath's on every voice:
> Those toward the truth with brain are blind or hate:
> The heart is cloven on a hidden choice:
> In which respect I still shall follow you.
> And, when I fail, know where the fault is due.

Andrew Hudgins

James
Agee

Lyrics

Child, should any pleasant boy
Find you lovely, many could,
Wind not up between your joy
The sly delays of maidenhood:

Spread all your beauty in his sight
And do him kindness every way,
Since soon, too soon, the wolfer night
Climbs in between, and ends fair play.

—

A summer noon the middle sun
Stunned me full of waking sleep
And spread me slack as stone upon
The grass in water foundered deep

There in that steep and loaded shine
Of hungriest life and crested year
To dream what plenitudes were mine
What fat futurities made near

When cold athwart these ripening plans
The shade o'erswam me like a sheet
Of draughty disappointed vans,
And lobbered beak, and drawling feet.

—

No doubt left. Enough deceiving.
Now I know you do not love.
Now you know I do not love.
Now we know we do not love.
No more doubt. No more deceiving.

Yet there is pity in us for each other
And better times are almost fresh as true.
The dog returns. And the man to his mother.
And tides. And you to me. And I to you.
And we are cowardly kind the cruellest way,
Feeling the cliff unmorsel from our heels
And knowing balance gone, we smile, and stay
A little, whirling our arms like desperate wheels.
—

Not met and marred with the year's whole turn of grief,
But easily on the mercy of the morning
Fell this still folded leaf:

Small that never Summer spread
Demented on the dusty heat;
And sweet that never Fall
Wrung sere and tarnished red;
Safe now that never knew
Stunning Winter's bitter blue
It fell fair in the fair season:

Therefore with reason
Dress all in cheer and lightly put away
   With music and glad will
This little child that cheated the long day
   Of the long day's ill:
Who knows this breathing joy, heavy on us all,
   Never, never, never.

A Song

I had a little child was born in the month of May.
He croaked and he crowed from early in the day.
He sang like a bird and he delighted to play
And before the night time he was gone away.

Little child, take no fright,
In that shadow where you are
The toothless glowworm grants you light.
Sure your mother's not afar.

Brave, brave, little boy,
Angels wave you round with joy.
Soon through the dark she runs to you,
Soon, soon your mother comforts you.

Description of Elysium

There: far, friends: ours: dear dominion:

Whole health resides with peace,
Gladness and never harm,
There not time turning,
Nor fear of flower of snow

Where marbling water slides
No charm may halt of chill,
Air aisling the open acres,
And all the gracious trees

Spout up their standing fountains
Of wind-beloved green
And the blue conclaved mountains
Are grave guards

Stone and springing field
Wide one tenderness,
The unalterable hour
Smiles deathlessness:

No thing is there thinks:
Mind the witherer
Withers on the outward air:
We can not come there.

Sure on this shining night
Of starmade shadows round,
Kindness must watch for me
This side the ground.

The late year lies down the north.
All is healed, all is health.
High summer holds the earth.
    Hearts all whole.

Sure on this shining night I weep for wonder wandering
        far alone
Of shadows on the stars.

Now thorn bone bare
Silenced with iron the branch's gullet:
Rattling merely on the air
Of hornleaved holly:

The stony mark where sand was by
The water of a nailèd foot:
The berry harder than the beak:
The hole beneath the dead oak root:

All now brought quiet
Through the latest throe
Quieted and ready and quiet:
Still not snow:

Still thorn bone bare
Iron in the silenced gully
Rattling only of the air
Through hornleaved holly.

The Happy Hen

(To Dr. Marie Stopes et al., and to all scientific lovers.)

His hottest love and most delight
The rooster knows for speed of fear
And winds her down and treads her right
And leaves her stuffed with dazzled cheer,

Rumpled allwhichways in her lint,
Who swears, shrugs, redeems her face,
And serves to mind us how a sprint
Heads swiftliest for the state of grace.

I loitered weeping with my bride for gladness
Her walking side against and both embracing
Through the brash brightening rain that now the season
    changes
White on the fallen air that now my fallen
                the fallen girl her grave effaces.

Dedication

To those who in all times have sought truth and who have told it in their art or in their living, who died in honor; and chiefly to these: Christ: Dante: Mozart: Shakspere: Bach: Homer: Beethoven: Swift: the fathers of Holy Scripture: Shelley: Brahms: Rembrandt: Keats: Cézanne: Gluck: Schubert: Lawrence: Van Gogh: and to an unknown sculptor of China, for his god's head.

To those of all times who have sought truth and who failed to tell it in their art or in their lives, and who now are dead.

To those who died in the high and humble knowledge of God: seers of visions; watchmen, defenders, vessels of his word; martyrs and priests and monarchs and young children and those of hurt mind; and to all saints unsainted.

To those unremembered who have died in no glory of peace, nor hope nor thought of any glory: to those who died in sorrow, and in kindness, and in bravery; to those who died in violence suddenly, and to all that saw not death upon them; to those who died awake to the work of death; to those who died in the dizziness of many years, not knowing their children for theirs; to those who died virgin, or barren; to those who died in the time of the joy of their strength; to those who took their own lives into the earth; to those who died in deadly sin.

To those who in their living time were frustrate with circumstance, and disadvantage; to those who died in the still desire of truth who never knew truth, nor much beauty, and small joy but the goodness of endurance; to all those who in all times have labored in the earth and who have wrought their time blindly, patient in the sun: and to all the dead in their generations:

And especially to Joel Tyler, and to James Agee my brave father, and to Jessie Tyler that became Mother Mary Gabriel, faithful maid-servant of the most high God, and to Emma Farrand, the wife of Joel Tyler.

May they rest.

To those who, living, are soon to die: and especially to Via my wife, and to my mother, and to my sister Emma and to David Preston her husband, and to Gladys Lamar Agee my father's mother; and to Hugh Tyler, and to Paula Tyler, and to Erskine Wright, priest.

And to James Harold Flye, priest, who befriended my boyhood with the wisdom of gentleness, and to Grace his wife; to Edwin Clark Whitall, priest, patient in all his life; to Dorothy Carr; to the leniency and wisdom of four men, and to the scorn of another, who teach at Exeter Academy; to Theodore Spencer, in gratefulness; in love, to Arthur Percy Saunders and to his wife Louise and to their children; and to a dozen friends, who know their names.

To Mark Twain; to Walt Whitman; to Ring Lardner; to Hart Crane; to Abraham Lincoln; and to my land and to the squatters upon it and to their ways and words in love; and to my country in indifference.

To the guts and to the flexing heart and to the whole body of this language in much love, in grief for my dulness and in shame for my smallness and meagreness and caution. May I in time become as worthy of it as man may become of his words.

To those living and soon to die who tell truth or tell of truth, or who honorably seek to tell, or who tell the truths of others: especially to James Joyce; to Charles Spencer Chaplin; to Ivor Armstrong Richards; to Archibald MacLeish; to William Butler Yeats; to Pablo Picasso; to Albert Edward Housman; to Stephen Spender; to Roy Harris; to Albert Einstein; to Frederick Burrhus Skinner; to Walker Evans; to Diego Rivera; to Orozco; to Ernest Hemingway; to Scott Fitzgerald; to Arturo Toscanini; to Yehudi Menuhin; to Irvine Frost Upham; to Robert Fitzgerald.

To those who know God lives, and who defend him.

To those who know the high estate of art, and who defend it.

To those who apprehend the dread of the magnitude of the destinies, and of the common conduct, of human kind, above all things known or earthly sought: and who as their hearts are able live toward the glory of the beauty, and in the shadow of the fear.

To those who suspect in every man, in the instant of his getting and thenceforward, how he is dignified among created creatures, how in him the world's whole harm and the world's whole good are met in the breath of God: and how in that instant he is given a mind to know and, though he be all one mechanism, freedom in his conduct before his creator.

To those who likewise suspect that hunger insatiable of the keeping and the enlargement and the knowing of being wherein he is conceived, wherein he lives, which in its appetites he may somewhat govern, and whereby he is wholly governed in all his ways.

To those who, beholding what man is, for love and for grief of what man should and may never earthly be, detest into madness man as he is and was and shall be, and all his works.

To those wiser who do not despise man in his doom, nor in the nature of his nature.

To that nature of man in earth which out of man's necessitudes, and delusions of necessitude, has wrought the societies and the nations of man, and his laws, that make a whore of justice, and his labors in the soil, and his workings of metal and stone and fibre and fire and light to his good use, and the contrivance of his ornament and entertainment, and his ways of good conduct and politeness; and his sciences; and his philosophies, and his religions, and his arts: and which interweaved these in the troubles and the nobilities of the flesh, and made them all into a structure no generation may deface, or destroy, but it will build again: so that in all the wraths of our hope and need we are compelled forward and forever newly into a same darkness of unperfect practice.

To that nature of man in earth which has wrought this time upon us.

To all pure scientists, anatomists of truth and its revealers; in scorn of their truth as truth; and in thanksgiving for their truth in its residence in truth.

To all scientists and inventors of convenience and rapidity, and ways of health: in thanksgiving for their reductions of human pain, and labor, and unhealth; and in scorn for the same: since in the right end of their busyness we would all be healthful and undesiring as animate stones.

To those men who, of all nations unhindered, to all nations faithless, make it their business to destroy concord and to incite war and to prolong it, for their profit in the commerce of armament: to those governors of nations who, in full knowledge of this, visit upon them neither punishment nor restriction nor disapproval, but are accomplices, exhorting and deceiving and compelling the men for whose good life they rule deliberately into death, and death's danger, and the shattering of flesh and spirit. Of these merchants and of these rulers may the loins thaw with a shrieking pain, and may there be slow nails in the skulls of each, and may lost winds of plague unspeakable alight like flies upon their flesh, here in this earth and by public arrangement, to the sweet entertainment of all men of good will: and in their death may the vengeance of God shock their flesh from their bones, and their bones off the air, and all that was of them be reduced to the quintessence of pain very eternal, from moment to moment more exquisite everlastingly, by a geometrical increase: unless by improbable miracle they repent themselves straightway and for good.

To those who will not see that there is a disease of cupidity, and love of the fatherland, and pride, and the good heat for valor, upon all human flesh, which builds these men their conveniences, and makes them easy of heart in murder as a grocer selling greens: and it is a disease which may hardly be cured.

To those who are sure they can cure it.

To those merchants, dealers and speculators in the wealth of the earth who own this world and its frames of law and government, its channels of advertisement and converse and opinion and its colleges, and most that is of its churches, and who employ this race and feed off it: to those among these rulers and these owners, these shapers of general thought, who decry these merchants of war: that they examine curiously, and honestly into their own hearts, and see how surely and to what like extent they in themselves are blood-guilty; and how and in what manifold ways they are more subtly and terribly and vastly accountable than for life blood alone: and that they repent their very existence as the men they are, and change or quit it: or visit the just curse upon themselves.

To those who think that any, or much, or all this condition may be a little, or much, or wholly changed. And to those who think that any one man is wholly guilty.

To those who have been deluded of their dignity as men and of their good knowledge into the practise and advancement of transient matters: to those whom love, or despair, or mildness, or magnanimity, or greed; or cloudiness of mind congenital or premeditated; or the strict allegories of the scientists, have thus deluded.

And especially to those whose souls are enraged that have beheld those practised and gravely cumulated idiocies which, since this race began, have been committed of man on men, for personal avarice or for national aggrandisement, lawlessly and by sanction and process of law; idiot children of that voracity which is the living strength of all men, and which may be changed in its courses for good or ill but never one jot altered in itself; those idiocies which have ever been and ever will be and are most obscenely now strong in the distinguishment of man from man, and strong to secure man's hatred of man and his privation, and dulness and blindness to truth, and eternal condemnation to wretchedness and all disadvantage. To those who have seen or suffered this condition, and who are fooled into the hope that it may be essentially changed. And into the hope that the cleansing of this state or its demolition and the establishment of a state new forged, and all discoveries of science applied, will do any greater service to man than to level and ameliorate the agonies and the exigencies of his living, to his ease, and into the ignorance of a contentment in earth and in the stuffs of the earth: to the blinding of his heart still further toward right knowledge of himself, and to the exasperation of those real agonies unbeheld, and in no time well beheld, of his ignorance before the mask of his destiny and before his God, where no knowledge nor ease of earth may help him.

And, knowing well that in this earth society, and law, and industry are the natural and indispensable necessities of man's earthly doom, earnestly to the hope (which can not be hope) that from this overthrow and change to come shall arise a race which, knowing concord in earth's least noisome commonwealth, may likewise know humility before God.

To those who will not watch into the mere shadow of death and behold the supremacy of man's ignorance over all man's knowledge. To those who will not see that there in that shadow is truth. To those who will not watch toward it, valuing it above all things in earth and valuing all things of earth in the thought of it.

To those among the murdering class who intend, and understand, no evil. To those among the murdered who grieve that they will murder many innocent men.

To all those who labor.

To those many who are indifferent to all semblance of truth; and to those millions who fear and detest it, and whom no change of state shall change.

To those who would not tell truth merely, but clearly in the hearts of all this people: for they crown a great impossibility, for which to die, with a mean crown and impossibility, and are somewhat mistaken.

To Leopold Bloom, and in his mildheartedness to all mankind.

To those who would be kind, and live quietly in the joy of their peacefulness.

To those who are more evil than kind.

To those dubious of evil, and of good.

To those who too surely distinguish them.

To those who have built this time in the earth in all its ways and who dwell in it variously as they may or must:

farmers and workers and wandering men and builders and clerks and legislators and priests and doctors and scientists and governors of nations and engineers and prisoners and servants and sailors and merchants and soldiers and airmen and artists: in cities amassed, and on wide water, and lonesome in the air, and dark under the earth, and laboring in the land, and in materials, and in the flesh, and in the mind, and in the heart: knowing little and less of great and little matters: enduring all things and most enduring living, each in his way of patience, who all, surely as a brook slopes into a deep cave and is lost, must die, into what destiny not one may know: to all these who live and who must die and to those whom they breed to follow them in the earth to live and endure and breed and die: to the earth itself in its loveliness, and in all this race has done to it: and to its substance, and to its children every one, quick or quiet:

And to that space and darkness of sky beyond conjecture and to the coastless coasts that curb it if any there be such and to the whirling fires and the dead stories of the sky in their progressions upon the dark:

To the Holy Catholic and Apostolic Church and to the reach of its green boughs upon the sky through Godhead into Godhead, and to its branches withering and withered and fallen away:

And to that which, climbing the very sap, may deathly cling and blight that tree: in hatred, in grief, in faith:

To the entire hierarchy of the natural God, of every creature lone creator, in his truth unthinkable, undimensionable, endlessness of endlessness: beseeching him that he shall preserve this people.

O God, hear us.
O God, spare us.
O God, have mercy upon us.

Not one among us has seen you, nor shall in our living time, and may never. We fumble all blind on the blind dark, even who would know you and who believe your name. Our very faith and our desire, which are our whole and only way in truth, they delude us always, and ever will, into false and previous visions, and into wrong attributions. Little as we know beyond the sill of death do we know your nature: and the best of our knowledge is but a faith, the shade and shape of a dream, and all pretense.

Nevertheless have mercy upon us O great Lord God: for as there is some mercy, and the imaginations of nobleness, even in this your creature, surely, surely there is mercy in you and honor and sweet might: and a way to hear, and a way to see, and wisdom, and careful love. Have mercy upon us therefore, O deep God of the void, spare this race in this your earth still in our free choice: who will turn to you, and again fail you, and once more turn as ever we have done. And make the eyes of our hearts, and the voice of our hearts in speech, honest and lovely within the fences of our nature, and a little clear.

Ann Garner

Like a stone set to mark a death, the bed
Leaned through the leaping darkness, gaunt and square
Against the firelight.
                    In her agony
Bent like a birch ice-laden, Ann Garner lay:
The silent woman by her in the dimness
Turned to the firelight, and said to the husband,
"She's laborin' hard; best set the plow beneath her."
Hips leant between the handles of the plow,
He thrust the flame-blue share beneath the bed.
And all the anguish flowed from her taut body,
Leaving her limp and silent in the darkness.
Then from the shadows the old woman walked,
Holding on rootlike hands the stillborn child.
The father drew the sheet to veil the eyes
That sought to pierce the leaping darkness where
Against the firelight, gaunt and square, the bed
Leaned like a stone set up to mark a death.

In harsh nakedness the earth upward thrusts
Its gaunt body, through the thin shroud of snow.
Above the rim of rocks, in the east,
Like a dull band of metal bends the dawn.
In the ice-clamped earth ring the shovels
And the ice-clamped earth leaps black
Against the sky.
                    At the grave, Ann Garner
Holds the child, in a fleece close-wrapped,
Close-locked in a strong oak box.

In a strong oak box close-locked
They lower him into the frozen earth,
Lower him among the frozen roots.
The earth drums loud on the box.
Loud ring the shovels, and the wails
Of the women ring across the barren fields.
The mother stands silent by the grave.

Here, on this height of pasture, where
The wheeling sky and turning earth
Convolute, grind;
Here, at the universe's core,
Here, on infinity's blind shore
Let him lie buried.

Here earth bereft again receives
Into her open womb, her babe;
Let the womb cohere:
Let the flesh of her babe become her flesh,
Let the blood of the babe to the hidden wells
Of life drain downward.

Let him live in womb and womb of earth;
In the swelling seed of every plant
Let him live.
Let him distil on rising mists,
Let him be blown along the sky,
Let him rise through womb and womb of light;
With stars at their birth
Let him again be born.

High in the dark looms of the sky, the wind
With gentle hands wove a fine web of snow
Which from those silent fingers flowed in silence
Downward, to trail across the stony hills,
Downward, to settle over the black fields.
And now about Ann, the white-shrouded fields
Swept outward into an oblivion
Of whiteness. On every side an even whiteness
Was all that Ann could see, save where the wind
Laid bare and dreadful some black, angled stone.

That night her husband held her in his arms,
Spoke a few broken words, and in the darkness
Waited in sorrowful silence for the weeping
That he could better bear and better comfort
Than speechless grief. But at his side she lay,
The white snows falling, falling in her soul,
Blinding her grief save where some twisted stratum
Of her soul's framework thrust up bare and black.
And thus she sat throughout the winter days,
Holding her grief within her as a woman
Carrying a child unborn cradles its presence,
And sits apart in silence, cherishing
Its unborn life in joyful solitude.
Her husband would sit in sorrow, watching her;
Watching her daily slip a little farther
From his desire, and sympathy, and love.

A few days later, answering his call,
The midwife came once more to minister
To Ann, in whom the unsuckled milk had curdled.

Down to the pond's edge the old woman led them,
Jeff with an axe and shovel. "Now start diggin',"
She said, "An' keep on diggin' till ye strike
The muck. Ye're sure to find one hereabouts."
He shoveled off the snow, and with the axe
Chopped out the ice. Kneeling, the woman peered
About, and with her fingers clawed aside
The frozen reeds. There, in the splintered ice
And twisted roots, she found a frog, frozen.
Cupping it in her hands, she blew upon it,
The white breath streaming from her twisted fingers,
Until life stirred within him. "Open yer bodice,"
She murmured. And Ann bared her aching breasts.
Then, holding by two legs the frog, she suddenly
Jerked, and the frog hung throbbing, torn asunder.
Against Ann's breasts she laid the trembling flesh.

That night Ann left her husband's side, and stole
Out to the barn. Through the warm dimness surged
The lantern light, and in the light she saw
The plow. She stood a moment, very still;
Then, grasping the smooth, lantern-shining handles,
And between the handles leaning, through the chaff
Deep-sifted on the floor, she pushed the point,
Webbing the dust with strange significance.
Deep in the barn a restless hoof struck wood,
Ann left the plow, and holding high the lantern
That shed the light in dipping circles round her,
She stopped before the stall where the black bull
Stood breathing silver mist into the darkness.
The heat rolled out against her from his body

As, wondering at the gigantic power
Low-swung and latent on those wide-spread legs,
Staring, she reached out with an eager palm,
And laid it, for a moment, on his body . . .
Then, with a shudder, drew her hand away,
And ran, with the lantern sucking all the light
From the warm barn, and from the stamping cattle.

After that night Ann was more strange and silent
Even than formerly. Through the steel-blue dusk
That joined so closely night with winter night,
She would sit spinning in the chimney corner,
The white thread flowing round the polished wheel,
The white snow falling, falling in her soul . . .
The ice thinned outward from the banks; the ice
Thawed upon birches pitifully bent.
From upland pasture the cold winter sky
Lifted its weight. And yet Ann sat and spun.
Always her eyes, dull as two stones, were fixed
On the white circle streaming through the darkness.
Thus passed the dim short days; and then in silence
Drawing the sheet to veil her eyes, she lay
Upon the bed which leaned against the firelight
Like a dark stone set to mark a death.

One night Ann woke, and, ear pressed to the darkness,
Knew that the world was called again to life.
Life poured against the walls in silent torrents . . .
The walls of wood, that locked her close within them!
She sprang up, and ran out into the night,
Blind in her running. Through the hissing pines

And out upon that naked lift of pasture
Where lay her stillborn child, she came, and there
Was caught in the wash and welter of two waves
Of life. From field and forest life welled upward,
And from the sky life fell like streaming rain
And lay upon the earth in a black flood.
Over the rock-rimmed pasture heights, the stars
Poured through the sky, and earthward from the sky
Struck silver rods of starlight, in black prisms
Of night.
       Ann stood a moment, hands upraised,
Then sank upon the grave, her body tense
Against the earth. And there she lay until
Dawn's white sun-bladed wings soared up the east.
Then standing up, beneath her feet she saw
Fields rear their arched brown backs above the mists,
Saw the wild foaming green on every tree.
She saw black cattle moving through the dawn
Up heights of pasture. Through the spreading dawn
Leaped a wild, silver wind, that circled round her,
Then gathered all its power and blew against
And through her, whipping her joy-maddened body
Into the riot and revel of its dance.

Now the blue plowshare surged in the broad fields,
The black earth, riven by the flame-like blade,
In sinuous furrows flowed behind. Ann watched
The plunging and inexorable plow,
Watched her husband guiding it, and when
The work was done, and over the quiet hills
The sky glowed greenly, stealing out alone,

Ann pressed her body to the raw, rich earth
And felt life swelling great against locked stones.
As the fields grew toward grandeur of the harvest,
Ann walked in silent joy through the tall grain
Silver and shadowy in the shifting wind,
Or stood beneath the dip of apple-boughs,
Long fingers searching out the ripening fruit
Let down in heaviness through clasp of leaves.

Now in the fields men cradled flashing scythes
Slanting in unison close to the ground.
The wheat sank ripe and rustling, and the women
Following, swept it up in golden armfuls,
Binding it on their hips.
                        But Ann stood by,
Chained to the earth by the ripe, gold grain,
Her body towering in the gold sunlight
Above the crash of wind-bewildered grain,
Above the harvest-work of man and metal.

On windy nights the apples thundered down.
The fields grew hard and black as the cold crept
Little by little down the bitter sky.
Ann saw the trees bleed on the earth their leaves,
And saw the rose-bush cower against the trellis,
And saw the rose lock all its life and color
Within a bitter berry, tremulous
On the bare bramble, in the icy wind.
She took her child and buried him again
High on the pasture, under the cold stars,
And bent her body to the whirring wheel.

When in the high looms of the windy sky
Fine veils of snow were woven and blew out
Above the naked fields, then in her soul
Fell the white snow, the blind and soothing snow.

As the years passed, the people turned to Ann
In doubt about some matter of their planting.
For with the years, Ann seemed to grow more learned
In all the mysteries of darkened moons,
Of hidden wells. And always at a birth
Silent and skilled she bent above the bed.
Always she moved among them like a ghost,
Her eyes as dull and fixed as two round stones.
But while the people round her bent their backs
Beneath the inexorable scourge of age,
Her body gained in stature and in strength,
Becoming every spring a little richer,
More flowing in its grace. And when alone,
Her eyes were still as water beneath mist.

All through the winter days she sat alone,
Spinning the white thread round the dark wood wheel;
At night she lay sometimes beside her husband,
Silent and grey and bitter, and more often
She stole out to the barn, and gazed about her
At all the symbols of the black earth's yield—
Plow, scythe, harrow—and lay down
To sleep among them, with the stamping cattle.
In winter she was never seen outdoors,
But locked her grief within the cabin's dimness.

But on the night
When Spring and Winter overlapped great wings
High in the sky, and like two eagles fought
For dominance below, she would run out
Into the flooding winds. And after that
She scarcely lived within the cabin's walls,
But with the cattle moving up the mountain
She walked along the streaming mists of dawn,
Until beneath the sun they burned to nothingness;
Then in the swaying dimness of the forest
She lay beneath the gnarled mountain laurel
Or on the cool and calm of fallen oak leaves,
And heard the rush of wind among the leaves,
The subtle writhe and shiver of an earth
Forever tortured by the myriad roots
Sprawling in darkness downward. And at night,
When the sheep whitely streamed down the bare hills,
When darkness welled down the wide peaceful sky,
And silence mourned over the misty earth,
She rose, and from the height of naked pasture
Watched the stars slowly swing across the sky,
Or brooded above the dark, wide fields that flowed
Into the starlight, cradling the life
That blindly moved within.

Life was in death:
The world rolled black and barren in its mists,
And life was locked deep in the sheathing snows;
Then wind and sun and rain came, like a lover,
Clasping the world in fierce, caressing arms,
And on her body lying, warm and undulant;
And all life sprang to meet him.

                                   And with life
Of her own life thus given each year's rebirth,
Ann came to look upon herself as earth,
And lying strained against the earth, cried out
In joy at sweeping winds, at the warm sun,
At the black rain that plunged into the earth.

And thus, as the years passed, she lost the rhythms
That govern human life, and seemed to live
More like a tree, or like the earth itself.
The only intercourse with humankind
She held, was at a childbirth or a funeral,
Or in the spring, when all the people turned
Toward her to guide them in their planting. Then
With strange serenity she moved among them,
Handling the simple farming implements
Like sacred symbols of fertility.

As long as Ann lived, all the countryside
Was rich in produce—as long as Ann lived.

Ann never would have died within four walls,
Her body stretched beneath a fear-clutched sheet.
She never could have died, save in some great
Catastrophe of all the universe.

On a night in moon-dark, all the people stood
Silent and fearful, at the soil's first breaking.
The horses loomed against the starry sky,
And Ann, behind them, stood a minute, gazing
Across the black earth, and the shrinking snows.

Then, grasping the curved handles of the plow,
She poised the point against the earth, and pushed.
The horses started forward, and the earth
Rolled back before the darkly gleaming blade.
Then, stepping silently along the furrow,
With a wide-sweeping arm she cast out grain,
And once more stood in silence, staring out
Across the windblown fields, the windblown stars.

Next morning, all the preachers of the country
Saddled their horses, rode to every cabin,
Stood in the doorway, clenching in white knuckles
A roll of scripture, and forewarned the people
That in the darkened moon, only two nights
From then, all in the dread of God should gather
To greet, amidst fearsome falling of the stars,
The blasting of evil and the doom of earth.
And all the people swarmed down the ravines,
And crowded the frame churches, and began
Even in early dusk, to wail and sing
And pray, and hear the preacher's exhortations.

Ann lay half sinking in the fragrant needles
Fallen beneath the pines. Above her rose
The pasture, straining toward darkening sky.
Faint upon the crest she could discern
The higher grass beneath which lay her child.
The pines hissed softly in the evening breeze,
And in the clear sky, one by one, the stars
Burned through. From far below in the valley
The slow bells of returning flocks rang out.

Then darkness, like a slow wind in the sky,
Settled upon the hills—
                              Down through the sky
A star streamed, like a golden rod that split
In half the darkness.

                              Ann sprang to her feet
And, running to the highest crest of pasture,
Stood, staring out across the world. Another
And yet another, and again a star
Streaked downward. All the heavens seemed to slip
And swoop and shuttle, weaving a wild web
Of gold across the sky. And then, through all,
Fell a great, burning sphere, and myriad stars
Around it—

    Sweeping above her wide black fields,
    Rending screaming air asunder,
    Into fields glowing stars
    Plunge with roll and groan of thunder.

    Down wide skies the golden plow
    Riving, cleaves a flaming furrow
    Wide for the seeds of a greater sowing.
    Whence comes the sower? Along the furrow

    Striding great upon the sky,
    Sweeping wide a flaming hand,
    He sows the universe anew,
    Advancing toward her pasture-land,
    Arms flexed above her, blotting the sky
    With body bent to the world's rim. . . .

Her husband found her on the heave of earth
Beneath which lay her child, in six oak boards
Tight-locked against the earth. Ann's hair was blown
Back from the hollow temples, in a way
To mould the head in savage eagerness
Which bent her body into one taut curve.

Clawing in jealousy at his swept beard,
He pondered the chisellings of lust
That so transformed in death the woman who
Had lived beside him silent as a ghost.
Then seeing that the clothes torn from her body
Were clenched in her own hands, he made all haste
To bury her before his neighbors, coming
And staring at that flared and joyful mouth,
Should nudge and whisper, and believe the thing
He knew could not be true. So, from his cabin
Returning with a shovel, he began
To dig, fearing to question the lustful mask.

He dug down through the grave where, years before,
His shovel rang out in the ice-clamped earth,
And digging, struck the box. He pried it open
And strangely gazed upon the fleece that wrapped
His child. Then, lifting in his arms his wife,
He lowered her among the broken roots,
And starting to replace the little box,
Stopped. From the fleece he clutched the crumbled
    bones,
And in Ann Garner's mouth he sprinkled bones,
And on Ann Garner's eyes he sprinkled bones—

Then gently laid the earth above her body,
And looked about him at the windswept dawn,
And slowly through the trees walked to his cabin.

A Chorale

Who, knowing love must die or live free-fated,
Free in your heartsearth headlong man created:
Who manly died and sealed from all perdition
        Our ill condition:

Your crown not God nor your great death retains you:
As you are man so man for man ordains you:
Who reign in man's regard O much forsaken
        Dear Christ awaken!

Range the blest hordes that rest in you around you:
Look down kind prince on treason to astound you:
See now sweet farmer what a wasting shadow
        Takes your green meadow:

How, love of self, fact, state, dream, art much prizing,
Men move in manners of their own devising:
How they kill truth to find out truth more nearly
        That's mortal merely:

How knowledge muffles wisdom's eye to danger:
How greed misrules: how greed's enraged avenger
Swears greed the equal prize for man's pursuing,
        And your undoing:

How many ways men build up man's disaster:
How all are armaments against man's master:
How surely soon comes toward without atonement
        Your disenthronement:

How cowardly those few that still exalt you
Worship their death while wildly men assault you:
How not one dares who knows what men intend you,
        Die to defend you:

Though you outreign our time which is an hour,
Yet you in us have put you in our power:
What God man builds in God His truth is ended
        Not well defended:

O Godsent Son of God our allsalvation,
Is faith so sickly slow to indignation
Your murderers against? Then faith betrays you:
        Your friends destroy you:

Your faith who gave your heart for our safekeeping,
Your love who sweated blood while we were sleeping,
If so these waste within this generation
        Death is your nation:

The time is withered of your ancient glory:
Your doing in this dear earth a pretty story:
O noblest heart fare well through the conclusion
        Of all delusion.

Great God kind God the deep fire-throated fountain
Of earth and funneled hell and hopeful mountain:
Of ghosted Gods the eversame survivor:
Of shoreless strength of peace the prime contriver:
If this your Son is now indeed debasèd
Among old effigies of Gods effacèd,
Blaze in our hearts who still in earth commend you:
Who through all desolation will defend you:
For we are blinded all and sick are swervèd
Steep among many Deaths who still would be preservèd.

Epithalamium

I

Now day departs: Upreared the darkness climbs
The breathless sky, leans wide above the fields,
And snows its silence round the muttering chimes:
The night is come that bride to bridegroom yields.

The night is come, that hallows as it harms,
That in perfection clothes the flesh defaced.
Now let the mother gather in her arms
The body that to other arms must haste.

For lo: from Oeta's wild and windflayed height
A star takes wing, soars up the wide arched sky.
And, from the constant fountain crest of flight,
Lowers on the marriage bed its prospering eye.

Still, with the glad impatient waiting o'er,
Weeping, with weak embrace, the mother shields
The maiden who is hers to guard no more:
The night is come, that bride to bridegroom yields.

II

Thick through the blended darkness slow-born dews
    distil,
Swell upon stem and stone, confuse the night.
Toward Hesperus still gazing poised fond above the hill
Now wind the glad torch flames, full blown and bright.

Soft through the sleeping meadows blind with dark
    and dew
We move, our torches shaking off the gloom.
We maim the soundless woodland, we bear our
    drenched yew,
We come to the marriage bed, the waiting groom.

III

Hesperus alone holds all the windworn sky,
Involves the bed in his steep, streaming light;
And dusts that ever in aloofness lie
Shudder to life, and marvel at the night.
Over the subtle ruin of her charms,

For from the sky now falls a holy dower
And the mute dusts, that swell with Hesperus' power,
Shall hold her joys and shield from all alarms.

IV

How proud in gentle modesty she lies
And greets her lover with stately tenderness.
No wanton glance, no false coquettish sighs
Betray her love, her sober eagerness.

No smile she grants, no blushes red confuse
Her pure flesh in its white tranquillity:
Quiet on her bed amid the glancing dews,
Queenly she waits in rich humility.

V

For that he, in whose arms you soon shall lie,
Not without guilt comes to a guiltless bride,
Still fear him not, but tender at his side
Recall his sorrow and his deep distress,
Recall his loneliness.

No boy has lived, but he has been his friend,
No maiden but has lain within his arms.
Hopeful of love fulfilled, he sought their charms,
But all the visions that his full heart cherished
In short time perished.

Through the dark depths of ocean and of sky,
Through all the world he pursued his endless quest,
And gathered every beauty to his breast:
But found no love, and sought on, unavailing,
His hope fast failing.

Now, with this night, his search is at an end.
The myriad blemished beauties you assumed,
That long were dead, late in enchantment bloomed.
Now, knowing all love and joy in you alone,
He takes you for his own.

So, wound him not with one misgiving sigh;
With his clear rapture let no sorrow blend.
Lo, holy Hesperus watches from on high,
His still fires round your lover's heart descend
And to rude passion put an end.

VI

Now the groom joins her, and the happy lovers
Bind heart to heart with close-encircling arms.
Hesper's clear benediction round them hovers;
The night is come that hallows as it harms.

O maids, through whose translucent masks of grief
Envious gladness gleams, for all her charms
Outshine your own, nay, Beauty's, past belief,
Your night will come, that hallows as it harms.

And youths, whose loving eyes feast and delay,
Though hope is gone, and holy vows are sealed,
Put off your sorrow, woo but for a day,
And night will come, and bride to bridegroom yield.

Over the lovers and the marriage bed,
Bare to the staring sky, the chilling dew,
Now close protection and concealment spread,
Clod upon branch, soft dust and sacred yew.

VII

Let no noise born of night come near their room:
No milk-eyed frog, with bubble-throated croaks,
Nor screaking bat, whose wings hook through the
      gloom,
Nor mournful owl, whose lost and dreary yell
The monstrous deities of the dark invokes.

Let no foul mist that cold above them trails
Settle upon them, smothering wrap them round.
But venom that the sweltering marsh exhales
Loose-coiled and prowling let the wind confound
And in the dry blast let its damp be drowned.

Let them lie safe: from every evil spell
That witches chant to sour true lovers' joys,
From the lank spirits night recalls from hell,
From ghost that gibbers, and from ghoul that wails,
From all malevolence the night employs.

It stands not in our narrow realm of power
To ward off aught that ever joy has marred,
But put off fear, for from this blessed hour
The stars, the sky, and all the earth, stand guard.

Root clenches root, dust into hard earth blends;
With bolts of stone the door's forever barred;
Across the wounded hill the long grass mends;
Around the lovers all the earth stands guard.

The twelve thongs of the wind shall lash and shred
The mists to air, shall soften, and retard,
And droop a rainy curtain round the bed:
Over the lovers all the sky stands guard.

Hesperus marshals all his myriad throng:
Down the deep night they gaze, with fond regard
And fateful, who shall shield them from all wrong:
Over the lovers all the stars stand guard.

VIII

'Tis time that we, who loved her through the day,
Whom Hesperus is urgent to bereave,
No longer should their rightful joys delay,
But fondly and forever take our leave.

Even now in tenderness the lovers pause,
And, for a moment, all is blind as night,
All, save their love, that, the next moment, draws
Them on to realms of measureless delight.

Knotted in secrecy, the sacred zone
From every harm the unharmed virgin shields:,
One may unloose the knot, and one alone:
The night is come, and bride to bridegroom yields.

Close in her kindly and untroubled arms,
He sets the zone aside, with gentle haste:
The night is come, that hallows as it harms,
And she assumes perfection, who was chaste.

Flesh and bright flesh he draws from off his bride:
Dust holds her wedding garment with the zone.
He who sets carnal nakedness aside
Knows the blank final bareness of the bone.

Now all is ready, now the happy bride
Lies unclothed as her lover, and on love
That long frustration and the zone denied,
Hesperus streams his sanction from above.

Now she yields all: her body to his own,
Her steadfast loving gaze, her mouth to his kiss—
All beauty and all love has never known
The ragged shadow of their radiant bliss.

Their love burns wilder, and the steady brand
Flares into furious and holy lust.
Their substance shivers and runs down like sand
Into the dust, and is one with the dust.

IX

For that the flesh arises like a wall
Between two souls, all love has known distress.
But they have conquered sorrow, conquered all
That clouded love: are one in nothingness.

Such nothingness remains, and yet is gone,
Looks upon all, and yet is void of sight,
Quickens the roots of every flowering dawn,
Coils in the core of every ripening night:

It breathes from steady water, is the pain
Of bursting seeds, the agony of earth
Shuddering out its life; streams down in rain
That causes and alleviates all birth:

X

When spring returns:—with every spring to come,
When the black worldseed buds and is full blown,
When all is singing that was frozen dumb,
Behold her children, whom no man has known!

When the long hill-grass hisses and interlaces,
When the tree stands aloof that split the stone,
When the leaves greenly stream in the wind-mad places,
Behold her children whom no man has known!

She who lies at the bottom of the night,
She who was flesh ere flesh revealed the bone
And bone relaxed to dust is deathless light:
And such her children whom no man has known!

XI

But still we stand, and they are scarce abed.
Scarce has their long and joyful night begun.
Now at their door the last yew branches spread
And hasten home; for night is nearly done.

Unformed and grey, heavy with lingering night,
Soft in its solitude stoops every tree.
All is submerged and blurred in fragile light
As at the bottom of a moonled sea.

Dispread among the hills, bemused and wan
Lie the night-tarnished half awakened fields.
The stars shrink back on white oblivion:
The dim sky loosens, and the long night yields.

Over the rim of mountains in the east
The daybreak, that through all the hours of night
Welled steady from the nadir, now, released,
Floods all the earth and sky with glassy light.

Wind flaws the shifting grandeur of the grain,
Pours through the green confusion of the leaves.
The mists become as air, our torches wane:
And once more Hesperus his dark hill perceives.

His strong and bright protection is as naught:
O'er lovers whom no darkness would dismay
O'er all enchantment that the night has wrought,
Merciless storms the overwhelming day.

XII

Quiet, forever free from all alarms,
They lie where light is strengthless to descend.
The night is come, that hallows as it harms:
The night is come that day may never end.

Sonnets

I

So it begins. Adam is in his earth
Tempted, and fallen, and his doom made sure
Oh, in the very instant of his birth:
Whose deathly nature must all things endure.
The hungers of his flesh, and mind, and heart,
That governed him when he was in the womb,
These ravenings multiply in every part:
And shall release him only to the tomb.
Meantime he works the earth, and builds up nations,
And trades, and wars, and learns, and worships chance,
And looks to God, and weaves the generations
Which shall his many hungerings advance
When he is sunken dead among his sins.
Adam is in this earth. So it begins.

II

Our doom is in our being. We began
In hunger eager more than ache of hell:
And in that hunger became each a man
Ravened with hunger death alone may spell:
And in that hunger live, as lived the dead,
Who sought, as now we seek, in the same ways,
Nobly, and hatefully, what angel's-bread
Might ever stand us out these short few days.
So is this race in this wild hour confounded:
And though you rectify the big distress,
And kill all outward wrong where wrong abounded,
Your hunger cannot make this hunger less

Which breeds all wrath and right, and shall not die
In earth, and finds some hope upon the sky.

III

The wide earth's orchard of your time of knowing,
Shine of the springtime pleasures into bloom
And branchèd throes of health: but soon the snowing
And tender foretaste of your afterdoom,
Of fallen blossoming air persuades the air
In hardier practises: and soon dilate
Fruits and the air together that shall bear
Earthward the heavied boughs and to their fate:
Wrung of the wealth and wonder they unfurled
By that same air: which air the sun deranges
To slope the living season from the world
And charge the world with snow that all estranges.
Watch well this sun, and air, and orchard green:
None stay these changes every man has seen.

IV

I have been fashioned on a chain of flesh
Whose ancient lengths are immolate in dust:
Frail though that dust be as the dew's mesh
The morning mars, it holds me to a trust:
My flesh that was, long as this flesh knew life,
Strove, and was valiant, still strove, and was naught:
Now it is mine to wage their valiant strife
And failing seek still what they ever sought.
I have been given wings they never wore.
I have been given hope they never knew.
And they were brave, who can be brave no more.

And they that live are kind as they are few.
'Tis mine to touch with deathlessness their clay:
And I shall fail, and join those I betray.

V

Strengthless they stand assembled in the shadow,
Blind to all strife and all to sorrow blind
Who reared the tower, who scored the April meadow:
Sheltered, they overshade my strengthless mind.
Those hands that gave their kind ungentle power
To summer's travail, autumn did not spare:
That mind which knew the clear, the intact hour,
Now is disparted on a changeful air.

The hands that ached to help are pithless bone
(Mind, mind, the harsh pain and the unalloyed:
What fruit you bear, that must you bear alone!)
The broken helmet nods around its void:
So I disclothe me of this shadow's blight;
And stand the axis of swift noon, sure night.

VI

Season of change the sun for distaff bearing
In your right hand and in the left large rains
And writhen winds and noiselessly forth faring
The earth abroad, and streaming wide your skeins,
When in unfathomed fairness you have clothed
The sea with quiet, the land with painless wealth,
Turn you to those who changelessly have loathed
All and their kind, and grant them peace and health:
The proud stone-parting ardor of the tree,

The glee of ice relaxed against new earth,
Joy of the lamb and lust of bloom-struck bee
Grant to the sick, stiff, spiteful, like fresh birth.
Let this new time no natural wheel derange:
Be ever changeless, thus: season of change.

VII

What dynasties of destinies undreamed
And truth to halt the heart does man descry
There, that so rarely has his heart beteemed
His eye to frankly watch into an eye?
The earliest marvelings only of the heart
Estranged of blindness of its living care
And from beholding Being held athwart
By narrowest shade, so deeply make him dare.
What truth we glimpse that each see other so
That stills our blood with horror of delight
Which once alone with other each may know:
Who swiftly changed recoil from that dread sight:
And how, if that were told, would change this day:
All human kind has seen, and none can say.

VIII

What curious thing is love that you and I
Hold it impervious to all distress
And insolent in gladness set it high
Above all other joy and goodliness?
Ignorance and unkindness, aspiration,
The weary flesh, the mind's inconstancy,
Even now conspire its sure disintegration:
Be mindful, love, of love's mortality.

Be mindful that all love is as the grass
And all the goodliness of love the flower
Of grass, for lo, its little day shall pass
And withering and decay define its hour.
All that we hold most lovely, and most cherish
And most are proud in, all shall surely perish.

IX

Why am I here? Why do you look at me
Triumphantly and lovingly and long?
When were we captured? When shall I be free
From your delight and this delicious wrong?
Not by your will I trust, nor by my own
I swear, nor any close device of reason
Are we engulfed by thicker walls than stone,
Mismated victims of unfounded treason.
Forbear, forbear to look at me with joy.
I would not do you hurt who will no harm,
But that sure smile I surely shall destroy—
Its covert meaning and its patent charm.
Awakened to our love's surprising hell,
Your dream-struck sleep befits it hardly well.

X

Wring me no more nor force from me that vow
Which lovers love to hear for reassurance;
Rest faithful in firm silence, which is now
Frail but sole bulwark for our love's endurance.
However mad, it is my heart's belief
That he who lies of love trumpets instruction
For anger and terror, scorn and doubt and grief

Swiftly to marshal toward our sure destruction.
Since, though we know naught else, we know love true,
When from the strict course which love's truth affirms
The sick brain swerves, to guiltless hearts accrue
Love's penalties and unpalliable terms.
If you love truly, speak the vow for me:
My lips can ill afford the blasphemy.

XI

For love departed, lover, cease to mourn.
Of flesh conceived, love fed upon our flesh
And of our agony and joy was born;
Whence often we have wept: weep not afresh.
How love grew strong and lovelier than we
Was all our joy, is for our solace still:
Woe though it was that wreck of strength to see
Thaw down and die, it was not by our will.
Our will? who sleepless and with anguished care
Plied every heartful balm and thoughtful cure,
Due rite of lust and precondemned prayer:
All which despite our love might not endure:
Because this forewrought evil has prevailed
Shall we mourn love and say that we have failed?

XII

Is love then royal on some holy height?
Thence does he judge us, thence dispense his grace?
There strike apart the darkness and the light
And shroud in light his sight-destroying face?
What are his laws? By what high-dealt decrees
Do lovers snared by all the laws of earth

Transcend the pain and cruelty and lost ease
That globes our globe, and soar to heavenward birth?
I have known love as lowly, full of lust,
Bent on contriving Godhead from the flesh,
Wrought of desire and waning through mistrust,
Starved in the sinuately carnal mesh.
Is there indeed a God who can redeem
The love we know as a dawn-tinctured dream?

XIII

Sorrowful or angry, hold it no way remiss
That, with the last gasp of love's healthless breath
(More cruelly stopped than with our latest kiss)
I would dissuade you from my imminent death.
The heart knows love exanimate of reason,
And your love thus beyond all reason dead;
The astounded brain, incredulous of treason,
Still must defy what heartful hope has fled.
Though the deliberate autumn air bereaves
With curious raveling all the rich-wrought earth,
The stringent winter through some idiot leaves
Outbrave defeat until the new leaves' birth:
When only (should that dubious spring renew)
Dying to live, I'll know my heart was true.

XIV

Not of good will my mother's flesh was wrought,
Whose parents sowed in joy, and garnered care:
The sullen harvest sudden winter brought
Upon their time, outlasting their despair.
Deep of a young girl's April strength his own

My father's drank, and draughted her to age:
Who in his strength met death and was outdone
Of pity and high purpose, grief, and rage.

Poor wrath and rich humility, these met,
Married, and sorrowing in a barren bed
Their flesh embraced in pity did beget
Flesh that must soon secure their fleshlihead:
But knows not when, on whom cannot descry,
And least of all could vaunt conjecture why.

xv

But that all these, so hopeful of their day,
Highsouled in joy and hungry for the fight,
Loved all too well such loving to betray,
And linked in love declined into the night
Whose dusk is flesh, whose dark is family,
Whose midnight is despair full-wrought from love;
Despair of strength and the soul's entity;
Opposed to noon by this thick world's remove.

And since I burn so wrathfully with joy,
And love also, as kindly as did they,
And so would fight, and so would not destroy
Night-hearted love that shows so proud a day:
I'll choose the course my fathers chose before.
And, with their shadows, pray my son does more.

xvi

How all a hurrying year was negligence,
Each meeting other as the casual merely,

In aimless fondness and the year's expense
Of much not seen and nothing sought sincerely:
Knowing such little truth, so lightly wearing
The small regrets of ill-established friends,
And our unmeasured liking meanly sharing,
And wanting yet evading all amends:

How, for all fear, that thing which dignifies
Our selves in each above those affable
So used its strength once that our helpless eyes
Killed and restored us in the fact in full:
How these things were, stuns and outstands my thought,
Now we are joined in all we scarcely sought.

XVII

I nothing saw in you that was not common
In some degree to any other friend,
Nothing that any amiable woman
Might not possess or by her wit pretend:
Only that we were straggling in our speech,
Uneasy in our liking, much as though
There dwelt such content in the heart of each
As needs must speak, but how it did not know:
True, this seemed strange to me, as well it might,
And did to you, yet neither had the art
To guess the truth and certify the sight
To the perceptions of the powerless heart:
Which now our selves so powerfully convince,
All the world else is idiocy since.

XVIII

The way the cleansouled mirror of a soul
Dreams in the darkened flesh and smoky breath
That only takes and tells the image whole
When all obstruction's wiped away by death:
So with our hearts that sleeping long have dreamed
Imaginations of celestial love.
Their flaws in each the other has redeemed
(True lovers such obscurities remove).
And now, but slowly, see our hearts awake.
The eyes unshut, the living sight shine clear;
How still each heart reluctant lies to take
The image of its image: though so near
We lie, that surely both our hearts perceive
Identities they scarcely yet believe.

Those former loves wherein our lives have run
Seeing them shining, following them far,
Were but a hot deflection of the sun,
The operation of a migrant star.
In that wrong time when still a shape of earth
Severed us far and stood our sight between,
Those loves were effigies of love whose worth
Was all our wandering nothing to have seen:
So toward those steep projections on our sky
We toiled though partners to their falsity
Who faintly in that falseness could descry
What now stands forth too marvelous to see:
Who one time loved in them the truth concealed:
And now must leave them in the truth revealed.

Now stands our love on that still verge of day
Where darkness loiters leaf to leaf releasing
Lone tree to silvering tree: then slopes away
Before the morning's deep-drawn strength increasing
Till the sweet land lies burnished in the dawn:
But sleeping still: nor stirs a thread of grass:
Large on the low hill and the spangled lawn
The pureleaved air dwells passionless as glass:
So stands our love new found and unaroused,
Appareled in all peace and innocence,
In all lost shadows of love past still drowsed
Against foreknowledge of such immanence
As now, with earth outshone and earth's wide air,
Shows each to other as this morning fair.

XXI

Who but sniffs substance gorges it, my soul,
Smothers digestion with stuffed appetite.
Disorders work in him and he is whole
One swill of dreams that all ways wreak him spite.
As arsenic can make a plant seem fresh
So are these hoisted dreams that are the flesh
A health not his and false and neverlasting
But loved once known which blinds with change
        and wasting.
So by my birth are you: wherefore this wry,
This raw corrective that alone outwrings
These doubly deathful healths: so thought we die
Yet so die not one coward but two kings.
So should we live, why then God lives also.
That was His Will which then will be our Woe.

XXII

When beyond noise of logic I shall know
And in that knowledge swear my knowledge bound
In all things constant, never more to show
Its head in any transience it has found:
When pride of knowledge, frames of government,
The wrath of justice gagged and greed in power,
Sure good, and certain ill, and high minds bent
On destiny sink deathward as this hour:
When deep beyond surmise the driven shade
Of this our earth and mind my mind confirms,
Essence and fact of all things that are made,
Nature in love in death are shown the terms:
When, through this lens, I've seen all things in one,
Then, nor before, I truly have begun.

XXIII

This little time the breath and bulk of being
Are met in me: who from the eldest shade
Of all undreamt am raised forth into seeing
As I may see, the state of all things made:
In sense and dream and death to make my heart
Wise in the loveliness and natural health
Of all, and God, upon the void a part:
Likewise to celebrate this commonwealth:
Believing nothing, and believing all,
In love, in detestation, but most
In naught to sing of all: to recall
What wisdom was before I was this ghost:
Such songs I shall not make nor truths shall know:
And once more mindless into truth shall go.

XXIV

Sure fortitude must disabuse my mind
Of all enlargements in unfounded hope
That I perceive whom fear of self made blind
My destiny constrained in my own scope.
All memory of magnificence of sound,
All grandeur and finality of word,
All nobleness some alien pain has found
That lives here painless, let them be interred.
Those men I worship and would stand among
In death well gained and reverently would greet,
Those immense souls have peopled mine too long,
And blown it broad with hope that was deceit:
And my poor soul, if aught it would create,
Must fast of these, and feed on its own fate.

XXV

My sovereign souls, God grant my sometime brothers,
I must desert your ways now if I can.
I followed hard but now forsake all others,
And stand in hope to make myself a man.
This mouth that blabbed so loud with foreign song
I'll shut awhile, or gargle if I sing.
Have patience, let me too, though it be long
Or never, till my throat shall truly ring.

These are confusing times and dazed with fate:
Fear, easy faith, or wrath's on every voice:
Those toward the truth with brain are blind or hate:
The heart is cloven on a hidden choice:
In which respect I shall follow you.
And, when I fail, know where the fault is due.

Permit Me Voyage

From the Third Voyage of Hart Crane

Take these who will as may be: I
Am careless now of what they fail:
My heart and mind discharted lie
And surely as the nervèd nail

Appoints all quarters on the north
So now it designates him forth
My sovereign God my princely soul
Whereon my flesh is priestly stole:

Whence forth shall my heart and mind
To God through soul entirely bow,
Therein such strong increase to find
In truth as is my fate to know:

Small though that be great God I know
I know in this gigantic day
What God is ruined and I know
How labors with Godhead this day:

How from the porches of our sky
The crested glory is declined:
And hear with what translated cry
The stridden soul is overshined:

And how this world of wildness through
True poets shall walk who herald you:
Of whom God grant me of your grace
To be, that shall preserve this race.

Permit me voyage, Love, into your hands.

Apotheosis

Lovers, make your kisses light,
    Weak, your embrace;
Keep passion cool and slight,
    A mask, your face:

Else (take heed) the sweet flesh slips
    Down from the dull
Dead bones, and lovers' lips
    Kiss but a skull.

1929

The Storm

The storm bows black on Stratham
    And strong through elm and ash,
Lashing the leaves to silver
    Low winds thrash.

From nought to like awakened,
    My puzzled soul is rent
By storms that know no ceasing
    Nor ever will relent

Till I bow black on Stratham
    And strong through elm and ash,
Lashing the leaves to silver
    With the winds thrash.

1929

The Shadow

The moon from shred to sickle grows,
Greatens to a monstrous tear,
Fattens almost overnight
Into a drunk o'erladen sphere:

Loses its rotundity,
Madly greets approaching doom;
Sickle dwindles into shred,
Shred melts grateful into gloom.

So, for a space, the Shadow will relent,
Befooling us with slow yet sure consent:
And, in due time, once more it will return,
Coolly to blot out what once more must burn.

1930

A Lovers' Dialogue

"O, let me set to this new wick,
Dry, and athirst for light, love's name.
So, we may watch the slow descent
Of wax ascend in steady flame.

For thus, virginity grows small;
Thus fails the firm and gallant flesh:
But, surely as it burns to naught
The soul arises, hot and fresh."

"No, I shall keep the wick unsinged:
The taper, white and whole and cool,
Shall never dwindle uselessly.
I shall preserve all."

                "Ah, sad fool,
You think a selfish beauty lasts;
Or, to bestow it whole were shame.
Hear: A sure death encases it
In one bright tube of instant flame!"

1930

The Rendezvous

The horn of resurrection
   Globes world and skull with jubilance of sound:
Perfect, my soul and flesh
   Resolve from living sky and deathly ground.

Ah, true to our appointment
   You join me, that together we may rise
To love's eternity . . .
   But tell me: what has saddened, so, your eyes?

"Only that you, who loved me
   Have waited long in vain new love to share:
Before the blazing God
   That cloudy love has burned to clearest air."

"Be sad no more; forget me
   As now I can you: lost in God your soul:
Me, love's thin fever
   Could not beguile from death's white ruinous coal!"

1930

Good Friday

High in Dodona's swaying groves,
High in the grey, the glimmering oaks,
Dodona's cauldrons, convolute,
Groan on the wind strange prophecies.

Among the whispering laurel roves
Great Pan, and on the tall sky, smokes
Of Delphi write; and now are mute
The graded reeds of Pan: he sees

Across the grey, the glimmering seas,
A leafless tree take barren root
On Golgotha; he hears the strokes
Of iron on iron, and his own hooves

The iron strikes through. Against two trees
Are driven his outstretched hands. Strange fruit
Hangs in the grey, the glimmering oaks,
Hangs in Dodona's swaying groves.

1930

Résumé

A year ago we wandered
The empty uplands wide,
Or in a leafy hollow
Mid wind-bewildered flowers
Forgot the turning hours:
Nor mused on what might follow,
But far too glad for thought
Strolled homeward silent, side by side,
Through veering sunlit showers.

Today, alone I wander
The empty uplands bare,
And where the earth is hollowed
I strew the flowers that wane
To thwart autumnal pain:
Nor muse on all that followed,
But sorrowful past all thought
Stroll nowhere, anywhere,
Through the tall, sunless rain.

1930

Sonnet

Death never swoops us round with sudden black.
No Gothic grin greets our affrighted groans.
Our flesh alone cries out, upon his rack,
Of snapping cartilage and splintering bones.
Secret and happy as a summer dawn
Blooms and releases its reluctant light
Full blown along the dusk, our souls are drawn
Beneath the vast and unrelenting night.

Even now, a serpent swells my living skull:
Its thirsty tongue, struck barbed through my brain,
Sucks all the cherished beauty dry and dull
As dust: and faint and failing is the pain.
I murdered joy, that your love might abide:
A precious skeleton lies at my side.

1930

Two Sonnets

We have been whirled once more into the realm
Of deathless night that blinds all other light;
Are free once more to grapple and enwhelm
The Ill it is our idiocy to fight.
Once more we strain our poor skull-bounded wits
Fast to control what Chaos could not stay;
The ceaseless twisting of a trillion spits
That offers us to each relentless day.
But as, for every day, the earth revolves
Thorough the solace of its steadfast shade,
So sure are we of death: sweet death resolves
All wrongs to naught, that had our hearts betrayed.
Therefore take comfort in this certain night,
And, for your peace, forget it may be night.

But if that death we long for be not night,
But night more pure by seventy times seven,
Ponder the agony of that delight,
The all-consuming clarity of heaven!
Made manifold by five celestial senses,
Five silver nerves strung helpless for the thrill
Of God's all-loving and God-loved cadenzas.
Further: there's no end to this holy day;
We are to God's eternal love betrayed.
His joy shall be our joy without dismay.
For holy light casts holier light for shade.
And we, who for long grief would spill our breath,
Will long for grief as now we long for death.

c. 1930–31

Description of Elysium

(*With Reservations*)

There is a pleasant land
    That has forgotten woe
Where time has lost command
    Nor flowers fear the snow,

Where silky waters stream
    That nevermore shall freeze,
And jewelled meadows gleam,
    And all the gracious trees

Spout up their standing fountains
    Of wind-beloved green,
And the blue-conclaved mountains
    Are grave guards and serene;

There brook and stone and flower
    Are one wide tenderness,
And they and a changeless hour
    Are touched with deathlessness:

Dear lover, lived we there
    Forever from tomorrow,
That loveliness we'd share
    We'd murder with our sorrow.

1931

The Truce

When, in such anguish of our love
As naught can temper or remove,
We lie beyond the hope of speech
And breathe our sorrow each to each,
One passion stands within my breast
Annihilating all the rest:
Lip and hand and flesh and bone
Are one large pity; pity alone
Is all my body can devise,
And pity gazes through my eyes.

Pitying, I seek your own,
And there, as still as any stone,
Pure as water wrung from flame,
Dwells a pity much the same.
While we look, those pities swell
Wide from double-sourced hell;
Deep and wide within that pool
Shines the pity of a fool;
Closer pressing, gazing, we
Know the idiot pity we.

So we look, and so love passes:
Take two flat quicksilvered glasses,
Press each to each the mirroring planes,
You naught can see, but much remains:
Bound in those flat and fragile walls
Stretch two bright and spaceless halls;
Beyond the glass, beyond the dull

Sponge of brain and box of skull
That straight and empty hall extends
And binds infinity's curved ends.

So much can our love attain,
Just so much, and that with pain;
Though we die to change the score,
Just so much, and nothing more.
Pity need not be the passion,
Though it be our private fashion:
Any single joy or grief
Turns the trick that cracks belief;
And the body's left behind
Whispering to the abandoned mind:

"So they look, and so Time passes
Withering o'er the glorious grasses:
Time shall ravel us asunder:
Mind's delight and body's wonder
And our shrewd-contrivèd lust,
Time shall wither into dust.
Where two pities stand displayed,
Shade shall mirror endless shade,
And they that have themselves forgot
Shall find no joy where self is not."

And the quiet mind makes reply:
"Many a time, before they die,
They shall hear our mutterings
And return to earthly things:
Try once more each sly device

We invent; none shall suffice.
Since much joy, but much more sorrow
Stands before their sunless morrow,
Vex not their unperplexity;
It cannot last as long as we."

1931

Resolution

This fire that lances me about,
This thunderous benumbing doubt,
This ocean-rooted sheer of rain
That brims the dark with smothering pain—

This wrack of murderous storm shall melt
Clean from the sky, and on the sky
The long-arrangèd stars have spelt
A fate no storm can set awry.

1931

A Poem of Poets

The harsh and profitable seasons pass
Bestowing each their own inestimable burdens,
Love its peculiar joy, love's end its proper grief,
Beauty its image, wisdom sought, its pain:

The mind so richly dowered, all withered are its
     guerdons;
Bloodless and sere and joyless, whose hour of green was
     brief,
They whisper deathly riddles to confused and dying
     grass:
Soon shall the mind be thoughtless, soon shall the autumn leaf
No more be bright memorial to the ancestral rain.

The mind is stunned, the tongue may find no word,
Nor in themselves may either find ever any thought
Beneath the awful instant of each high visitation,
Beneath the blinding and celestial fire,
Fit to do thankful honor to Him the fire Who wrought:
Wherefore with gilded praises and with false
     lamentation
We sing into the darkening sky too tardily to be heard,
Who soon shall be brought low to earth and that humiliation
Which gluts the oak with pride and burns the poppy with
     desire.

All seasons pass, once more they swerve above,
Once more the mind is granted the living fire to
     breathe,
Once more of green and holy and far-gathered leaves we
     fashion
Straitly implied with brief domestic flowers,
Pride, artifice, despair, our wild half-hallowed wreath:
To crown the mind with fame, and God with
     earth-bound passion,

Flaw truth with beauty, make a holy whore of sickened
    love:
Once more, and now forever, impends that immolation
Whence we shall rise to damn still other poets with half-blind
    power.

1931

A Parable of Doors

(*and of their construction*)

All things of life I term as many doors:
Entrance to each or all, that man may win
Who neither questions, nor no more implores
But that with mindless ease he be let in.

Such men are myriad and the doors swing wide
And smoothly they swarm through, who care not why,
Initiate to those mysteries most denied
Those who most seek them: such a man am I.

I would expound those truths unalterably
Flayed to strict harmonies no mind has sung.
Mindful that truths are founded axially,
By too much mind all hinges I have sprung:

For it was thus: I lunged the brutal mind
Shoulder to hinge post, since the truth stood there;
Which neither yielded nor have I repined,
But lunge and batter and am in despair.

I cramped all gates of love forever shut,
All beauty is for ever wrecked for me,
And God all spiked with brain, and there is but
One door, whose certitude the others flee.

That door is death: and though my chief assault
And shrewdest labor I've assembled there,
Dark hinges no conjecture may default
Soon shall devolve me on a doorless air.

1931

Delinquent

Neat in their niches with retroussé faces
The choir boys chant the chorale of the mass,
Suspicious sopranos and imminent basses,
Molding their mouths as a blower molds glass.
Hymning the high gods with oscillations,
As pliable lips adapt to the air,
Distracting the flock from divine occupations
By singing so loudly and looking so fair.
Limp in their linen that glistens and grates,
They ogle an octave with unctuous eyes,
Or lower shy lids as the organ abates,
Demure as a demon in cherub disguise,
Till troubled parishioners cannot be sure
So much naïveté's utterly pure.

c. 1931–32

Home Again Blues

Now we are home with Mom and Dad
  And huckleberry pie,
In fact the Things We Fought For:
  And now we wonder why.

For Mom is just a garter-belt
  And Dad is just a bore,
And as for good home cooking
  We had too much before.

And that, we guess, is what it means
  To be a U.S. Veteran.
We'll never fight another war
  Until they start a better one.

c. 1931–32

The Passionate Poet to His Love

Come live with me and be my love
Provided you think little of
Such stodge encumbrances as friends
Who keep their means for their own ends;

Granted we mutually agree
That yours was never a mother's knee,
Or, if the spiteful slime should bud,
Will nip the foetus while it's mud;

Provided you can smoothly be
Wife, mother or nonentity
As metamorphic moods require;
Provided, also, you admire

Nor ever dare to criticize
Each syllable that I devise,
And shall apprise me (though I know it)
Of my majority as a poet,

And, like four angels each with sword
Will guard the Inception of the Word—
If such persuasions aught can move,
Then live with me and be my love.

1932

———

When I was small delight and fear
Were eminent upon my blood.
Watched I but once into the sun
Great shadows walked my mind of God.

To watch but once among the stars
The broad-borne earth lie down to rest,
That was to know of what huge host
We were the shy and country guest.

And bird and brain and spring and fall
Were creatures of his kindlihood,
And wrong and right were freely ours
To screen apart as best we could.

But I, and wiser men than I,
Have since deduced much better sense.
My brain is very quiet and clear.
The shadows have departed thence.

And all our findings reassure
My wavering blood, my halted breath,
To strive and stream in careless health
From now until my day of death.

Before which there is much to learn,
And nothing, nothing much to know.
Wherefore bring madness for my brain.
And for my blood that childish glow.

c. 1932

Lyrics

I

Sad heart stray backward through the lifted shadow,
Glean the lost plantations of their heavy gear
Those things we knew when we and they were green
    and careless,
That now are ripe and rich, that now are past and dear.

II

No room: hard weather:
Two in the careless dark
Who nurse numbed love alive
Wince against the wall together.

Let the deaf storm drive:
Forget the glowing room: hark:
Curse neither world nor weather,
Time shall build you time together
And an easy bed
And a safe room
Big as the dark.

c. 1932

Class Ode, 1932

Now the winter is past and the storms of our youth,
    We who gather to part in our power
Long acquainted with dreams, seal our sight to the
      truth,
    Who shall labor to live for an hour:
Now the snows are withdrawn and the fields young in
      bloom,
    All that lives strains in strength toward the light,
And the comrades who halted in doubt and in gloom
    Depart drunk o'er the down-trampled night.

Ay, the sun rides the zenith and sunk under the earth
    Huddle midnight and winter and death.

But the smothering darkness that paled at our birth
    Shall return to reprieve us of breath:
And the oak shall be stripped, the bright furrow lie bare,
    The man wane, the tall shadow destroy:
We shall waste on that vast and invincible air
    And our valour be naught and this joy.

When the slow wheel shall turn, and our course shall be
        run,
    In the breath that the brave season brings,
Fallen flesh shall upwield from each husk to the sun
    And the wild strength of all sorrowless springs:
And all wisdom we wring from our pain and desire
    On this field between devil and God,
Shall resolve to a white and unquenchable fire
    That shall cleanse the dark clay we have trod.

1932

——

As you came through the far land
    Many speak well of
Saw you there, anywhere,
    My own true love?

You would know her, if you had,
    By her quiet eyes, and bright smile,
By her small breast and her soft step,
    By her wit without guile.

73

How shall I know your true love
     From another one,
Who saw many like her you speak
     When I was there, who are gone?

All dwellers in that far land,
     Their eyes are quiet, and bright their smile:
Their flesh is small and their step soft,
     And they have neither wit nor guile.

And are they never cruel,
     Never harsh nor unkind?
Do they never clench the hand
     Nor strike with the mind?

Nor hurt with the sullen glance
     And the bitter tongue?
And do they never know distress
     Who are lovers, and young?

Do they not contract the brow
     In silent rage?
Nor ever forget and hate
     And falter in age?

Oh, they are free from all these flaws,
The dwellers in that strifeless land,
They speak and think no evil there
Nor deal it with the heart or hand:

Their brows are smooth as ivory,
Their tongues are sweet as morning air,
Their hands are quiet as carven wood,
And neither anger nor despair

Shall move them more: young lovers lie
Freed from all malice and regret:
The aged hate no longer there
And no more falter and forget—

Oh, God himself made such a land.
To that sweet land I'd hasten now
Did I but know her surely there—
But cannot know: and know not how

To make my journey to that place:
Tell me, that I may see it soon:
Shall I obey the landward sun
Or seaward errors of the moon?

To get there soonest: do not budge:
Unbuckle with a knife
The slippery harness of the blood:
And thus race free of life.

And if your true love dwells not
In that far land you seek,
She will come, soon enough,
Next year, or next week:

All your search will be done,
    And all your despair:
You shall embrace in solid stone,
You shall kiss in shining air:
You shall be nor two, nor one, but none:
    But none:
And neither of you shall care.

                                    1932

Theme with Variations

Theme: Night stands up the east:
           Day glides down the west:
           Lax in his fur the beast
           The bird with brow in breast

           Yields each the addled hope
           That stood him sunward guide:
           Through all the shadow's scope
           The dew distends its tide:

           And all is strifeless quite:
           All free from all affray:
           And down the west falls night:
           And up the east fares day:

Variation 1

           Whole to the hollow shadow
           Commend your heavy brow:

All pomp of day put from you
And deep through darkness bow:

The margin withers of the morning dew:
Weighed clear the lands that loved this keep of
    shade
Now mount the noon beneath and meet for you
The terms wherein the round lands are betrayed:

The same, the deep dealt law that you debased
Into this bourne of death that makes you whole
Lifts up refreshed to lower these lands defaced:
All withered is the early dew:

Some high delirious meadow
Delivers the late letter of your mutual vow:
Peace: peace: be healed: all wholesomeness
    become you:
Your night is on you now:

Variation 2

    They that led the long loam open
    They that mouthed the meadow short
    They that scruffed the wry roots' sweetness,
        Beasts of this laborious sort:

    Sourbrained mule and horse meekheaded
    Grimbutted cow and dafteyed sheep
    Gristly hog and their gay children
        All have shut them whole in sleep:

Light, the jaws on bruisèd kernel,
Coffined quiet, the maulèd cud:
Quiet also the soft, the young ones:
  Shy the doomsday mounts their blood:

Variation 3

  The whistlers slick and chortlers
  The free the smart of song:
  The deft on wing in the wild white day
  Throng muttering shrugged and asleep nor
    stray
  The green boughs deep among:

  Safe from the shadowing high ways
  The latest wing is home:
  The eagerest wing that was abroad
  Is idle now and the wing outlawed:
  The happiest throat is dumb:

  Beneath the proud-armed buzzard
  The air slopes damp and blind:
  And hunched in tenting cumbrous wing
  He sleeps that leaned in a deathward ring
  His downright hand behind:

Variation 4

Where now the lizard and the rinded snake
That skipped and slurred their lengths and
     lusted in the heat?
Where the lean bugs that on the water break
Their rapid dances and each other eat?

The lithe-tongued butterfly where now is he
That chanced his bright wings on the unequal
     air?
Where the mean hornet and the sweet-groined
     bee:
Now they are under night how may these
     bloodless fare?

The reptile's eye is blue: the thready fly
Stands on the skin of water, he is well:
The tongue is furled and the fair dust not
     flawed and the wings shut high:
The stout bee grumbles in his paper cell:

1933

Sonnet

Now it is competent, our common heart
And we two fragments found to fit entire
And we two whom the long night held apart
Meet in the high wealth of the morning's fire:
With all predictions cancelled in the fact

And our rich insufficience satisfied.
I meditate those things our life has lacked:
Some things our love must ever be denied.
I am most envious of those careless years
When full of care we knew each other not
And green false love, false happiness, false tears,
Ripened this whole heart, which must wholly rot;
The dreamful heart that woke toward prime of day
Dreams now of dawn and darkly wastes away.

1933

Sonnet

Two years have passed, and made a perfect wheel
Of all that love can know of joy and pain.
All that lovers hope or dread to feel
We've felt, and are arrived at naught again.
On barren earth the sky has loosed its rain
Too generously: last year's abundant yield
Now straggles up, a green and scattered stain
Across the drenched exhaustion of the field.

So, let us leave off trying, now, to mend
A chain long broken; let us play no more
At being firmly bound: love's at an end
And cannot live again. Oh, set no stars
On other loves; all love's a ceaseless bend
From naught to naught: farewell: make fast your door.

c. 1933–35

———

Him we killed and laid alone
Is not sleeping in the stone.
Stopt in spices, shelved in stone,
He is not sleeping in that cell.
Death paid and living earned he walks
The spirals of our present hell.
Steep on whose terrific street
Shines the calmness of his feet.
Sulphurous around him glare
The maledictions of despair.
He looks out in that sad land
Those of whom that land was made
And for whose love his life was paid.
And granting each a cloven hand
Forth from the ruined realm of shade
Before God's light as I believe
Leads out Adam, leads out Eve.

1935

———

A low pit and sink of shade
And funneled dark I find me made:
Long has lapsed my laden sight
Sourceward down that floorless night:
Down the echoing soul's delusion
And the hooded skull's confusion,

Down my marrow into earth
Searching out my nether worth.
Deeper than my breath can follow
Silence falls beneath me hollow.
Naught of all I'd die to do
May I do, who find naught true
That's truely mine: I find me made
A cistern full of standing shade.

1935

———

When Eve first saw the glittering day
Watch by the wan world side
She learned her worst and down she lay
In the streaming land, and cried.

When Adam saw the mastering night
First board the world's wan lifted breast,
He climbed his bride with all his might
And sank to gentlest rest.

And night took both and day brought high
The children that must likewise die;
And all our grief and all our joy
To time's deep end shall time destroy,
And weave us one, and waive us under,
Where is neither faith nor wonder.

1935

A Poem for Brahms' Death-Bed

Fulfilled, the long, the well-wrought life,
Accomplished, the undeviant years:
The man who took his work to wife
Dies in high grief of childish tears:

Still with the Death-Tears on his eyes,
New beauty starts about his brow:
Humbly astounded, he descries
Those lordly ones his comrades now:

One grandly gay, serenely strong:
One who walks shining in his grace:
One gross-cheeked in huge natural song:
And one with stunned translated face:

These catch in theirs his own wide hand,
They hail him brother: (and the large air
Burns with the music of that land,
The sovereign music that is there).

1935

Period Pieces from the Mid-Thirties

I: *Fellow-Traveler*

Mumsy told me not to play with all those rougher girls
    and boys
And perhaps that's why I sleep today with a girl in smelly
    corduroys:
And if only Mumsy had kept mum about the sunnier
    side of God,
Perhaps I wouldn't have left Him on the seamier side of
    the sod.

Mumsy you were so genteel
That you made your son a heel.
Sonnybunch must now reclaim
From the sewerpipe of his shame
Any little coin he can
To reassure him he's a man
(Though personally he would hate to
Try it out on that potato
Known still to reactionaries
And a few misguided fairies
Of the older-fashioned kind
As the human heart and mind).

So, Mumsy, I go round and round the streets and the
    hired halls,
Shouting by mouth and placard the dialectic is the balls,
Taking at every chance my ideological temperature,

Hoping to God it's normal but keeping-my-mouth-
    wide-open-to-make-sure.
I still like William Shakespeare but I see just where he
    lacks,
I'm the staunchest of admirers of Miss Clara
    Weatherwax.

I'm a Friend of the New Masses I'm a Friend of the
    New China
I'm a Friend of the New Spirit that's Alive in Carolina.
I'm a Friend of everything on earth from shit to
    sasparooly
Except, of course, the bosses, you, Mom, Jesus, and
    yours truly.

II: *Agrarian*

In the region of the T V A
Of the cedars and the sick red clay
We've discovered a solution
Neither Hearstian nor Roosian
In the embers of a burnt-out day.

When the world swings back to sense
(But the world is *so* damned dense)
An indisputably Aryan
Jeffersonian Agrarian
Will be settin' on the ole rail fence,

Swaying slightly with a hot cawn bun,
Quoting Horace and the late John Donne,

He will keep the annual figures
Safe from the prying eyes of niggers,
And back his Culture up with whip and gun.

And every single solitary region
Will cultivate its own religion,
And we'll each frame our millenium
In an open-air proscenium
Unbedunged by any non-indigenous pigeon.

III: *Regionalists, Nationalists*

Sugah-foot, set on mah knee
   Ah wants to ax you sumpn
What is dis stuff de Regionalis'
   An Nationalis' is dumpin'?

Hit smell so quair I can't make aout
   Rightly, honey, was it
Food fo de privy-chickens, gal,
   Aw foe de tuhkey buzzahd.

Dey shaouts fer Nawf dey shaouts fer Saouf
   Dey shaouts fer EEs un Wes
Haow all de othah-places may be good
   But dey's de bes':

An' dem as outgrows his neighbahhood
   Sets up a laoudah scream
Abaout de hull dang countryside
   An' de American Dream.

What was dat dream', sweetie-pie?
    Dey ain't no one will set
'N let on was it skeery, sweet,
    Or jist de old fashion wet.

Dis Engle feller, naow, he looks
    A powful nice young man:
Folks tell me haow he's jist a flash
    In D. J. Adams' pan.

But I wouldn' take nobody's word
    Fer nufn, not no mo,
Not sence dey give de Plitzah Prize
    To Striblin's book, de Sto'.

IV: *Georgia Democrat*

Ah calls awn ivah dimocrat dat's sho nuf dimocratic
    To rally raoun en smoke dem varmints outen aouh
        nation's attic:
Ah calls awn ivah fahmuh dat ain't got no adjucation
    To git a Prez-Dent dat can plaow undah dis hull
        dadbuhned nation.

Ah calls awn ivah thenkn mayun dat liaks mah briaght
        reyud galluses
    To sind a mayun to da Whiat Haouse dat sets daown
        awn hahduhned calluses
An ah calls awn ivah dipaty, Ku Kluxah an ex-sojuh
    To keep dem niggahs in day place till ah gits back to
        Jojuh.

mid-1930s

Three Cabaret Songs

I
These sultry nights, dear
   Pour me some gin
Turn down the lights, dear
   (Now we begin)
We've got our rights, dear
   (Some call it sin)
And you've Nothing to Lose

Nothing to lose
   And lots to gain
Good deal of pleasure
   (Some call it pain)
No way to measure
   But in the main
   I'd nothing to lose
   (And less to choose).

Nothing to lose
   And lots to gain
No news is good news
   (Say that again)
Who'll take this flooz-
   y out of the rain
I've nothing, nothing, nothing to lose:
I may as well pay that devil his dues
   I've nothing whatever to lose.

II

Wake up Threeish,
    Clean up the sink
Air out the bedroom
    Pour out a drink
Drink to the daylight
    Sit down and think
I'm Open All Night.

Go to the movies,
    Stroll in the park
Watch the kids playing
    Wait for the dark,
Then I remember
    A fellow named Clark
I'm Open All Night.

Buy me a mirror
    Make up the bed
Order the White Rock
    Get my self fed
Prink up and sit down
    And wish I was dead
I'm Open All Night.

III

NO BODY SEES
(In the spring time pairs)
OR KNOWS
(Like us like those like these)

OR CARES

(Like the wood wind preening
Masking and mowing
And the following flow of the garrulous leaves

O the trees yield soft
And the leaves flow green
And the young pairs roll beneath and between
And ever and oft
Under ledge in loft
A boy stoops proud and straddles a queen.)

Do you think THEY SEE
    (their midparts spitting)
Do you think THEY KNOW
    (of the pitiless knitting)
Do you think THEY CARE
    Of the dark flesh fitting:

The life to be
The hurt to grow
The flower to blow
On a ravenous air:
Which does not see
Nor know
Nor care:
Saw it the end it would not dare

Nor grow (no, no!)
    Nor be (Tee-hee! For)
No Body Sees Nor Knows Nor Cares!

undated

_____

You green in the young day
Pledge tall things to your pride,
You brave in thought of woe
Walk in the bullet's way;

You murderers for gain
Be gainful while you can,
You that would change the score
Be merciless and destroy:

You lonely that must mourn,
You that are made of cheer,
You that all harms have borne,
You that see no thing clear:

You woman and you man
Bridegroom and happy bride
Find out your truest joy
Grown true your mortal tide:

That pride and greed and anger,
Bravery and grief and love;
All death holds deep in danger
Death shall not quite remove:

And so may this ill-tuned remark
Of mine, and many others,
Run light among the living
When I am in the dark.

mid-1930s

Now on the stunned floor of darkness
Grateful in their element,
Lovers, poets and dreams awakening
Wrangle, shine, and learn content.

Windlassing their chiming buckets
Heavily on the unspeaking mouth
Out of wells of worlds forgotten
Dreams allay the daylight drouth.

Strolling stone and taciturn pavement,
Swift behind the spearing light,
Sorrowfully poets deliver
Resolutions of the night.

Lovers eating love of either
With insatiable hand
Lie like starfish on the seafloor
Through this wild and wicked land.

1935

A Song

Give over, give over,
Whose grievance ever yet delayed the sun?
White smiles the dew, the summer's work is over,
And your fond love, your lover,
Is no man now, and now's another one.
Give over, give over:
What profits an arraignment of the sun.

1936

Two Songs on the Economy of Abundance

Temperance Note: and Weather Prophecy

Watch well The Poor in this late hour
Before the wretched wonder stop:
Who march among a thundershower
And never touch a drop.

Red Sea

How long this way: that everywhere
We make our march the water stands
Apart and all our wine is air
And all our ease the emptied sands?

1936

—

Now I lay me down beside
My friend, my girl, my love, my bride.
And where you bless another bed
My hand sustains your lovely head.

Though we spend this night apart,
By an illimitable art
Separation, quite undressed,
Yields me your look, your laugh, your breast.

O should our thoughts lie down to sleep
I pray the Lord our love to keep.
If love should die before we wake
I pray the Lord our love to take.

1936

Lyric

Demure morning   morning margin   glows cold flows
    foaled:
Fouled is flown   float float   easily earth before
    demurely:

Chanced gems   leaves their harbors
Sparkle above leaves   whom light lifted

Drilling in their curly throats   severally   sweet
      ordinate phrases
                  Smooth ancestral phrases:

Teaching: touching: sinuous disunison.

Drinking: drafting: each of all   serenest pleasure.

Bring floral earth your breast before her,
Afford your breast before the morning.

Demurely,   the early margin:

Fouled is fallen   flower   flower   Fearless earth before:
      serenely:

1936

FROM **John Carter**

Like Byron, I'll begin at the beginning.
      Unlike that better bard, my lad's a new one,
Expert in charm, supremely so in sinning,
      Nevertheless he differs from Don Juan
In ways enough to set your brain to spinning.
      For how he differs, read the books ensuing:
For this time's being and this being's place
Are both beginning and in medias res.

In medias New York State stands the Homestead;
    In medias that, in medias modest gloom,
Is a large room: in medias that, a bed:
    In medias which a man and wife consume
The night with pleasure: for they're three weeks wed,
    And the bride's trained at last: in medias whom
George Carter labors lovingly: deception
Is not my aim: you're in at the conception.

A present fad, especially in sex,
    Flatters the reader's fond imagination.
All right as art, it has its ill effects,
    I find, in causing curious agitation
Miles wide the subject: Reader then suspects
    Author of plans to undermine the nation—
All cleanmindedness; and maybe takes his pleasure
No more in reading, but in legislature.

I know a type the governors of whose eyebrow
    Are most unstable, and whose inner cheek
Pockets his tongue, while, "This is pretty sly now,"
    He neighs, and gives your elbow a smart tweak.
I'd dearly like to know the reason why, now:
    I use my tongue to taste and kiss and speak,
And never use my eyebrow, even to ogle;
And *my* verb for his action is, "to groogle."

"*Groogle*: to love subversive wit and wary;
    To draw the mouth down; lecherously to leer;
To be a slob and something of a fairy;
    To snout out filth in every word you hear.

Synonymous with pseudo-literary."
     I think our word has onomatopoeia:
Anyway, Webster'd thus anatomize it:
I coin, define, with all my heart despise it.

Let subtleties rejoice within their due.
     I find no subtlety in new-ploughed earth,
Whether that earth be meadowland or you,
     But honest beauty and fit cause for mirth.
Both at their best are far between and few,
     But sweetest in conspiracy toward birth,
Whether the pair be nomad, noble, citizen,
Or the young Carters ready to beget a son.

However that may be, they knew a joy
     As strong as the arched sea, as common, too:
Knew pain, mirth, beauty: what could ever destroy
     That speechless fire of liking twixt the two?
Naught, at this hour: the elements of their boy
     Knit, and enwrought their cloudless love, and knew
All evil and scorn straightway: but they two wept
Their utmost joy, quietly embraced, and slept.

Even as they slept beneath the unslumbering dawn
     There was a stirring, and the spiteful slime
Sucked livelihood from her most kindly brawn,
     Huddled its core, began the gradual climb
Whence ageless life forth from the dust slow drawn
     Flowered into grass, beast, man: abiding time,
Our hero framed his black chill clarity
From his first hour with blood of charity.

Warning: I've given my boy his proper start;
        He's on the fire; we'll all have months to wait.
And if the last two stanzas please you not
        As too obliquely stated, obfuscate,
Abstruse, or what not, blame it not on art.
        You'll find abundant justice, soon or late,
Whether you're priest, pimp, matron, child or spinster,
If they seem strained, or even a trifle sinister.

Meanwhile, the young wife slumbers in the arms
        Of her young husband, and he slumbers, too;
The incipient contriver of dark harms
        Slumbers (I guess) where harm cannot pursue;
All prospects please but one. That one alarms
        Me plenty: namely, reader, slumber you?
For now we face the hideous jaws of Lull.
I'll do my damnedest not to make them dull.

Of course for you, reader, the problem's easy:
        I must write on; it don't have to be read.
Some poets' alchemic bellows are so wheezy
        They turn the best of gold to their own lead.
God spare me that: my first aim is to please ye—
        If this part fails, why take a look ahead.
You'll find large portions (this I swear to you)
Will please most anyone, I don't care who.

For my intention's to diversify
        My subject matter and my manner too:
I'll use all styles from Lardner to blank verse if I
        Can make the grade, which should please you
                and you

And even you, in turn. And my own 'erse, if I
        Fail, I shall duly kill, and up to you
I leave that wager, choice, and member also:
Lots like to "take the literary pulse," so.

Now that demands another parenthetic
        Remark or two; I'll cut it fairly short.
If that last stanza seem a bit splenetic,
        It's just because it makes me fairly snort
To see the anemic, phthisic and emetic
        Verdicts doled out in Literary Court.
There's too much sugary simpering civility:
When a book's rotten, roar it down as guilty!

Critics, you overrate our sensitivity.
        We'll take it, *we'll* receive it on our chins,
Except those lads who, through your own proclivity
        For stuffy talk upholstered with glazed chintz
Are frail, though sweet; and if you're wrong, we'll give it ye
        Back where it came; the sharpest penman wins.
Besides, I think good tooth for tooth invective
Far more effective than a Mild Corrective.

Observe the hallmark case of Leonard Dash.
        Sad as a schoolchild, pained in adolescence,
His frail deistic dreams went all to smash
        With worrying sick about the Actual Presence;
First Mumsy, then Our Lady was his mash;
        Myrrh was his mouthwash, frankincense his *essence*:
And he bothered more than any sane youth ought to
Whether 'twas nice to wear lace on his cotta.

He had a secret vice, as you and I did,
     But being shy, indulged it rather more;
And when he'd made his penance and had tidied
     Himself, and lay and heard his roommate snore,
And felt that granulation of the eyelid,
     The brain grow corky and the gums get sore,
He prayed to God to save him from that doom
The Rector's said was sure to happen to'm.

Meanwhile, he tried *Tom Jones* and couldn't keep on,
     But did like Poe and Bierce and Baudelaire,
De Musset and La Forgue, nor went to sleep on
     De Quincy and the Book of Common Prayer,
And Celtic Crepuscules, nor counted sheep on
     A lot of things that needed country air.
(Some of these things are more than pretty good:
The trouble was this Artist's attitude.)

His literary likings, then, were Gallic.
     He also liked black candles and Debussy,
Old prints and Wagner, heavily metallic
     Brocades. His best friend's name was Hubert Pusey.
They learned all holy cults sprang from the phallic,
     And ecstasized o'er every iterant pussy,
And read translations from the Ancient Persian,
And did lots more things which are my aversion.

You see the trouble was, he needed Girls:
     For while it's fine to give one's God His due,
And thrilling fun to gather up those pearls
     Spurned one's rough schoolmates, but good as new,

To watch that wonder which the dawn unfurls
      Exclusively to one (or maybe two),
One horrid urge can drive one to despair
Who wastes one's flagrance on the desert air.

It flurried Leonard frightfully at times.
      At nights, he thought of one thing and another,
Of sweet-fleshed maidens bred in palmier climes,
      Also of Jesus, Hubert, and his mother.
So finally, when he'd hoarded enough dimes,
      He snuck to Boston . . . Well, I guess I'll smother
That little incident (which nearly threw him):
A friend has come, I want to read this to him.

The friend has gone, and so have twenty days;
      So have several stanzas, and my manuscript.
So have my wits. My mind is in a maze.
      All energy and all high hope have slipped
Smoothly away. And thus the poet oft pays:
      Imagination's subtle skein is snipped
When by weak will or strong against his liking
He shelves too long his too young undertaking.

By all I love, I'll make no alibis!
      Blame my own mind or curse the circumstance:
It matters little where the trouble lies
      Or by what slant collusion or brute chance
I could, and can not now; for I despise
      More than I pity that egregious nance
Who gilds with tears the wasted morning-glory:
Therefore, for good or ill, on with my story.

There were no red plush draperies round the bed,
    There were no silver mirrors on the ceiling,
No dizzying reek of musk involved his head,
    No candle flames assayed the dusk's unsealing,
No stifled streams of hidden music bled
    Their muted loveliness round love's revealing:
All lavender lore that Leonard had devoured
Defaulted him the night he was deflowered.

Her purple locks were silvering through the dye,
    Each royal breast was like a splotched melon,
Her teeth were caulked with gold: I'll not deny
    Hers was an epiderm to gaze, not smell, on:
Her guts were bunchy and each marble thigh
    Was like an o'erlain pillow: and a felon
Glowed on one knuckle of one square-nailed hand:
She smacked his withers and said, "Ain't love grand?"

Squelching his bitter nausea he replied
    That yes it was, and fumbled his cravat:
Ruth cast her dress and kicked her mules aside:
    He turned his back: gulped: glanced at his hat:
Stepped from his trousers with a desperate pride
    (Ruth smoked and watched him sidelong as she sat)
Sank shuddering on the bed he would abuse:
(And Ruth undid the laces of his shoes).

True lust will triumph over indigestion:
    (God moves in a mysterious way, I hear,
But here and now I think we'd really best shun
    Such thoughts, and say biology is queer)

So Leonard, when he'd understood her question,
    Put his five dollars on the chiffonier,
Porous-Knits on the floor and self upon
The whore: and in two shakes the job was done.

Just how this influenced Leonard's later Work
    Or why I told or what it did to him
I can't quite know: I blush to say, I shirk
    These chores which keep the Artist's soul in trim.
But here's the point: I'll leave it in its murk,
    You may extract it, if so runs your whim,
Artists will understand, for it's in style:
The Frailest Plants take root in what's most vile.

Artists who can't refer to such a night,
    Like Artists who affect complete monogamy,
May rest assured their genius is but slight,
    Unless, indeed, they find a touch of sodomy
More fits their fancy—but a leaden blight
    Sickens my spirit way down deep inside o' me:
The poor pure Minors—for the work's so poor all
Of those who choke their souls with staying moral!

Well, back to Leonard. Things were very strained,
    He found, when he divulged to Hubert Pusey
His wonders and his horrors and regained
    Some sort of balance (having thought it Juicy
One moment, Sin the next); Hubert was pained
    Beyond all words, he stammered, "I accuse"; he
Rushed from the room, wept out his shock and fear,
And three weeks thence contracted gonorrhea.

I'm rather sick of Leonard; so are you.
       And so, although there's much more to be said,
I think I'll chuck him one more verse or two
       (It's more than he deserves) and so to bed.
Such lads as he, alas, are more than few,
       And more than few of them, now be it said,
Hover their spark, as he did too, and fan it
And, even as Leonard, publish *Gold from Granite*.

Or some such title. What a nice slim book!
       Those grim grey covers stamped with slender gold.
You've seen the dedication? Give a look:
       "This young book TO MY MOTHER, never old."
How charming, and see here, the printer took
       Such pains to choose a type precise and cold,
Biting yet delicate, but none would do,
So a young German flute designed a new.

Some of the poems have six lines to a page!
       They promise easy reading for weak eyes.
Can poets achieve nobility of rage,
       Be witty, sensuous, passionate and wise,
When soul's subjected to this stringent gauge,
       And mind reigns at the juncture of the thighs?
Poems, like the sea, might lunge and weave and flow.
Are these poems oceanic? Jesus, no!

Or do they even approach the mathematical?
       Sinews and guts demand a skeleton,
And it's a matter highly problematical
       Whether elastic flesh or rigorous bone

Is most important. This remark is what I call
        Something which poets had better leave alone,
Remembering, though, that naked bone is death,
And boneless flesh is soon unpleasant breath.

But these have neither bones nor face nor bowels,
        And they are neither fish nor flesh, but foul:
Squeamishly juggled consonants and vowels
        Raise the Soul's Paean to a placid howl—
Oh, scores such bland and well-upholstered owls
        Squat in their stumps and make believe to prowl
Wide through that blind and noisome realm of night
Which they term Life, being short or nil of sight.

Some might be richly leaved and lordly trunked, if
        They could work out a good excuse for life:
One Neo-Arthurian scales the dread subjunctive
        Gathering samphire with a neat desk-knife;
One farmer's verse in splendor might be dunked, if
        His hired man, farmer, or the farmer's wife
Shut up their dismal dialectic squawking
For even five lines, and let *him* do the talking.

One Californian's vision is gigantic
        In images alone; his line's too long;
His people start at scratch and end in frantic
        Rape of wild beasts or brothers, which is wrong,
I'm told, who never tried it, and romantic
        Beyond the scope of measured sin and song:
Great tragic poems have less unleashed ferocity,
More rhythm and much more temperate reciprocity.

One, of a great but singular ability,
>Contrived expert symbolic bellyaches,
Toiled thence to higher, drier debility;
>Now, Anglo-Tory-o-Classico, he shakes
(Solemnly slow, with infinite gentility)
>Stark cypress and jewelled pomegranate, and makes
From drifted talismans and ripe archaics,
Rich, rigid, undecipherable mosaics.

By this time it is nearly seven-thirty.
>My poem thus far is heavily digression,
Some critical, some moral, some just dirty
>(If so you think) some riding my profession
(If such I have); if anyone feels hurt, he
>May find cross-irritants in the procession
Of stanzas which ensue, for there he'll see
(If I'm in luck) himself, and you, and me.

For we're Americans, for which we may
>As well thank God, since that's our pleasant doom.
It just ain't done, forever or today
>By taking thought to backslide to the womb
And thence emerge, to everyone's dismay,
>In other times or as a gaudier bloom,
As Negro, nabob, Greek or Jacobite,
Elizabethan or New Muscovite.

Homer and Plato and the dirt are one,
>Shakespeare and Swift inform the deathstruck
>>flower;
The wild black breadth of Russia's but begun
>To rear its green illimitable power;

Our Western Zero shrewdly chokes our sun:
      Yet, in this brief and steeply shadowed hour
Ere flesh deserts and earth adopts the bone
There's more to do than sit and make sweet moan.

The piebald earth revolves and still the rain
      Silverly stoops on tower and field and hill;
Still man is man and still the man-wrought pain
      Is studious to hurt and waste and kill;
Still there is loveliness and love of gain
      And love and love of hate and therefore still
The farmer knows a newness in each seed
Nor need the poet deplore a gorgeless reed.

Murder and stealth and raw-eyed revelry,
      Popular noises, mineral-hearted light,
Flawed lust and pure and sweet inanity
      Of general sleep: these breed beneath the night:
Such is the stifled turmoil of a sea
      Flattened by fog of steep and stormless height:
Thus for the comedy of this our age
Behold the wide, dark and unpeopled stage.

This breadth of earth is crumpled into stone
      On east and west, and broad on either hand
Two seas are spread, and on the east alone
      The daybreak leans and soon will find the land:
The gleaming looms of gloomy brine are grown
      Sure in the light, and now discovered stand
Islands and toiling ships and the long shore
Fire-born, sea-suckled now and evermore.

Over one badge of city on broad ground
    A breathing silver brightens and is day:
The dark falls westward and a subtle sound
    Climbs with the clear surf's everlasting sway:
Immortal morning, furiously crowned,
    Walks shod with music on her earthly way:
Music of bird in branch and scythe on wheat,
Of startled engines and a million feet.

Now the wide-bellied ocean sunward drawn
    Swollen with light against full morning moves,
Flexing its glad and multitudinous brawn:
    While steeply from the carved Atlantic coves
Flare the wild gulls who silvering catch the dawn
    On wind-hooked pinions and in flashing droves
Shift and dissolve in swivelling flight and squeal
Stooping toward waves to strike with glittering heel.

Levelled to earth the broad loud-chattering blade
    Drops the gold barley backward from its stance;
And where the clamorous roiling knives invade,
    Grasshoppers spangle up in desperate dance,
Showering aslant to patter disarrayed
    Into the unhurt grain and unknown chance,
While still the blade whirrs forward and around,
Narrowing the green sphere of their scatheless ground.

Just so the light's unvanquishable blade,
    Whetted to darkness on its eastward edge,
From dew-shot turf and reed and songless glade
    As lately from bald isle and seaward ledge

Upwields the birds from out the deafened shade,
        And that keen height of purest air they fledge
With wings splayed wide and wide the thrilling gorge:
Blind, toward the unapproachable high forge.

Oh, blind they scale that brightest air and keen,
        Free up the unceiled porches of the day,
Beyond the shadow of the night's cruel screen,
        Beyond the solitude of birds of prey,
And, as a crested fountain stands serene,
        So stand the birds above the earth's dismay:
Who, as the dawn glides past, once more decline
Into the green world and the steep dayshine.

1932–36

In Memory of My Father

(*Campbell County, Tenn.*)

allegretto

Bluely, bluely, styles from stone chimneys crippling
        smoke
of hickory larch and cedar wood of elm of the white oak.

The quell night blues above. The quell night blues:
Branchwaters, the black woods, begin to talk.

The blue night blacks above: Lamps:
Bloom in their glasses and the stars:

Splinter and glister glass. Warmth:
Slopes from the pigsty. In the barn pale hay,
Tusseled in teeth, darkness, a blunt hoof.

The black night blinds above. Tell me was ever love.
so gentle in
the hand . so tender in the eye. was ever love. :
more lovely to the loved.

The secret water smiles upon herself; the blue cedar :
stands in his stone of smoke.
Mile on mile in mountain folded valley fallen   valley lies.
Eyes fixed on silence small owls preach forlorn forlorn:
The metal thrill of frog and cricket thousands in the
        weltered grass:
Swinging his chain   the whippoorwill   the
        whippoorwill   the answering chain:
Deepchested from his bowstring   a big frog bolts
        response :

                swinging his grieving chain

Cry, lonesome preacher : choir, shrill creatures of
        enamored dew:
amorous water, parley, elapse : slow stars, display your
        edges :
effortless air : love in the neat leaves   the neat leaves :
        gentle
colony in your green harbor   throes of a common
        dream   throes in
the leaves, and quiet : sweet tended field, now meditate
        your

children , child , in your smokesweet quilt ,   joy in
    your dreams,
and father , mother : whose rude hands rest you mutual
    of the
flesh : rest in your kind flesh well :

And thou most tender earth :

Lift through this love thy creatures on the light.

1937

Lyrics

I

Remember limber thunder in the deaf : the metal
    tasting air:

    Cities like silly medals lay : wind
    Flashed the whole forest pale.

Spasm and blindness blanched and the bunched cloud
    Delivered his blue columns.

Remembering thunder : deliberating in the shadow cold :
    the fuse air

    The paltry medals on that pitiful breast : the wind
    Violating the pale forest crest:

    Twittering blaze, the hunched cloud
    Voided : and slept aloof : the miles

Restored into the sun : the clean sun
Sheened in his scope:

Remembering unlimbering thunder in the deafness and
the tinder air:

The pinned and pendant cities : in the woods
A whole year's generations struck one white:

Collaborative, and determinate thunder:

II

Soft heaven shuts: at length the latest
Plaintiff is silenced and the ample south
Absorbs him unlamenting:

Here, moreover, subdued, the seed
Meditates and shall publish the usual flower:

And he, restored, bounding on bloodied twig,
Schemes out his spiritual music.

III

His subtle throat is broken on the air;
        (Reproachfulness, outbreast the wind)
That pointed eye, narrow hands, the fluted bone
        Lie with the forest fall.

Yet with the year, shall, with the wrinkling leaves,
    The frail shell break, the fragile monster breathe,
        and,
Falling, wing find air: and talk to god
    Much like his grandfather in his time.

IV

Tonight sweet heart I think in graves of the wild earth
        forgotten,
Straws of old harvest whom the sun ignores,
Bones, and their bran, congratulate.

I do not think they pity us.
They pity less than they are glad.

All that was ardent and which now is air:
Warms round our wrestling here.

V

Heal, hardy air, harm in earth.
And yield these lungs the while to breathe
It takes to whisper out that worth
Whose cloudy forehead you enwreathe.

VI

Not for your ease or pleasing was the air
Mild, the while past, and loving with the earth.
What for the seethe of health up breadth of summer
I cannot guess, but doubtless not for us.

Cruellest and dingiest of the squatters we
Who wring and craft and tease this field apart.
From the huge kindness of their kingdom's edge
The citizens peer seldom but to hide.

However, there are harms about the heart
We never dealt us, but can only serve.
Serve them then as we must, to further harm,
And help what can; and meantime let who will
Lift on this glimmered dark his joy, his small surmise,
     while,
Serious and unregarding, with stiff hands the heavens
     Rust and unwreathe the world.

VII

Squared behind intellectual hedges:
Bloodhounds and rifles arranged to guard:
Be sure: subtly, how cheated faith avenges.

Make the mind only a little too hard:
Suspect too fearfully the irrational:
Your feet will break through tunnels under your yard.
You will be unseated by an unforeseen international.

Have you surely added it up to the right amount?
Shall florid history never split your pot?
Have you taken the animals thoroughly into account?
Are you sure it is still yourself you dream of or not.

VIII

Your end's to end forever
    War's wrath, the rotted laws.
But man in his last anger
    Shall kill for larger cause.

IX

Tears are the touchers of that secret earth
No alien rains attend; be therefore tears;
Grieve, and your holy land accords you mirth;
Pity brings wrens of the most batflight fears.

X: *A Nursery Rhyme*

Glimmer, glimmer, universe
Whom storms of mysteries immerse:
Nebulae not grieved for Zion
The blown seeds of a dandelion:

How I wonder by what rules
Beyond the touch of local fools
In the anarchic spring unborn
Whose front lawn you shall adorn.

What immeasurable child
Shall your burning have beguiled
Before another picks you dry
And puffs your promise down the sky.

In what city shall that be
And in what strange vicinity.
(Hark my friend we've had our day,
School is out, they're on their way.)

Gods snub each other on our back stairs
The ancient time contemned as snares.
Our galaxy, so runs the hope,
Is mirror for a telescope.

Curved brightness is a beveled jewel
Examining minute renewal.
All things undreamt, one atom's core.
One spark of sand, its endless shore.

There thrive fish the dark sea down
Unsuspicious of our town.
We each are lumps in a same leaven
And Friday's print amazes heaven.

XI: *Education of the Prince*

He must strike down his father's cedar shadow:
Sever his mother's terrible and sorrowing mouth:
Abandon, under their stone labels in the charted meadow
His tired friends, and start the journey south.

Follow the man on the hill with the fire on his back:
Outbrave the monstrous lady of the woods:
Speak dialect, snap twigs deceptively, destroy his name:
He must make the dark journey under the hollow sea.

1937

Sunday: Outskirts of Knoxville, Tennessee

There, in the earliest and chary spring, the dogwood
    flowers.

Unharnessed in the friendly sunday air
By the red brambles, on the river bluffs,
Clerks and their choices pair.

Thrive by, not near, masked all away by shrub and
    juniper,
The ford v eight, racing the chevrolet.

They can not trouble her:

Her breasts, helped open from the afforded lace,
Lie like a peaceful lake;
And on his mouth she breaks her gentleness:

Oh, wave them awake!

They are not of the birds. Such innocence
Brings us whole to break us only.
Theirs are not happy words.

We that are human cannot hope.
Our tenderest joys oblige us most.
No chain so cuts the bone; and sweetest silk most
    shrewdly strangles.

How this must end, that now please love were ended,
In kitchens, bedfights, silences, women's-pages,

Sickness of heart before goldlettered doors,
Stale flesh, hard collars, agony in antiseptic corridors,
Spankings, remonstrances, fishing trips, orange juice,
Policies, incapacities, a chevrolet,
Scorn of their children, kind contempt exchanged,
Recalls, tears, second honeymoons, pity,
Shouted corrections of missed syllables,
Hot water bags, gallstones, falls down stairs,
Stammerings, soft foods, confusion of personalities,
Oldfashioned christmases, suspicions of theft,
Arrangements with morticians taken care of by sons in
        law,
Small rooms beneath the gables of brick bungalows,
The tumbler smashed, the glance between daughter and
        husband,
The empty body in the lonely bed
And, in the empty concrete porch, blown ash
Grandchildren wandering the betraying sun

Now, on the winsome crumbling shelves of the horror
God show, God blind these children!

1937

Sun Our Father

Sun our father while I slept
You lifted like a field of corn
The smiling and the peaceful strength
Of those that are the race new born:

The infant future waked in you
Once more, and at the world's rich breast
Drank the day's courage and lay down
In fearless and refreshing rest:

And while the russian field you raised
Dreams in the starflung shadow's keep
You wake these backward lands to work:
Good work to do before we sleep.

1937

Summer Evening

Bandstands every tuesday evening
Bring us to the drawling square:
Braid, glad horn, blunt drum, commend us
Each another, shed of care.

Locusts with enthusiasm
Celebrate the spended day:
In the dappling shadowed porchswing
Love finds out the usual way.

Children are composed this season.
There is hope among us yet.
Hope can cut the roots of reason:
And the sorrowful man forget.

1937

Lyric

From now on kill America out of your mind.
America is dead these hundred years.
You've better work to do, and things to find.
   Waste neither time nor tears.

See, rather, all the millions and all the land
Mutually shapen as a child of love.
As individual as a hand.
   And to be thought highly of.

The wrinkling mountains stay: the master stream
Still soils the Gulf a hundred amber miles:
A people as a creature in a dream
   Not yet awakened, smiles.

Those poisons which were low along the air
Like mists, like mists are lifting. Even now
Thousands are breathing health in, here and there:
   Millions are learning how.

1937

———

As in a woodland rarely,
Still to the ear, the eye,
One leaf, in its own soul's temblor
Signals, talks, so I:

So in my devastation,
Rarely, the shaken soul
Tells me at throat and eyelid
The legend whole.

Only, how long since the wind
Made a wooden sea, since a tear
Sprang like a seed. Since the leaf knew
I am not there to hear.

What do you bring into this woodland
Which makes it all one denial, one frown?
What do you bear from the unshadowed
Realm, that you would here lay down?

Lay down, be cleansed of, silently,
Here, where the patient mold drinks in
Like ants, leaves, rains, the years,
To kill and bury immortal sin.

Never hope it. None can help.
Where you search, comfort veils
Cryptic as a negro. Every
Prayer's a heartbreak. Desire fails.

1938

To Walker Evans

Against time and the damages of the brain
Sharpen and calibrate. Not yet in full,
Yet in some arbitrated part
Order the façade of the listless summer.

Spies, moving delicately among the enemy,
The younger sons, the fools,
Set somewhat aside the dialects and the stained skins of
    feigned madness,
Ambiguously signal, baffle, the eluded sentinel.

Edgar, weeping for pity, to the shelf of that sick bluff,
Bring your blind father, and describe a little;
Behold him, part wakened, fallen among field flowers
    shallow
But undisclosed, withdraw.

Not yet that naked hour when armed,
Disguise flung flat, squarely we challenge the fiend.
Still, comrade, the running of beasts and the ruining
    heaven
Still captive the old wild king.

1941

On the Word *Asleep*

Asleep, perfected, you would never believe
Harm of a one of them. That stirring hand,
That leg, might clasp, endear, be brought across
An enemy, as gently as a wife.
How God must grieve,
Watching in all this shadow land
The flinching vigil candles of this countless loss
In night's nave each a life:
Who groans, smiles, murmurs, quiets; then on the horn
Transpierced, assembles upward, and reborn,
By all that skill and bravery crowns him with
Works, while he wakes, to put himself to death.

1945

On the Word *Kingdom*

In that kingdom no one cries.
No one doubts, for no one lies.
No son ever dreads his mother,
Nor no brother envies brother.

Families, there like nearby trees
Spring and shelter, and the bees
Groan among the cloudy flowers;
Angels, each a soul devours.

There continually the smile
Of the heart that knows no guile.
There, untroubled, people greet
Death like an old friend in the street.

1945

O my poor country I have so much hated,
How can I hate you now your doom is near?
How still revile a soul so desolated,
Or hold your hideous sickness else but dear?
Ruthless in force but not so ruthless quite
To use it wholly in the last thin chance
History affords, against eternal night;
Kindly, but so roared round by circumstance
Of greed, self-love, self-righteousness, the shattered
World groans its anguished last against your ear,
And you are merely petulant and flattered;
Incurable through pity, love, guilt, fear:
A dying grandmother, babbling of a ball:
Take her just so, Death; let her enjoy it all.

1945

Dear Father

Dear Father:

Monday evening, fairly late—
Too late for serious work, not late enough,
Quite yet, to lay the insomniac's nightly bait
For sleep, with cards, trash-reading, all such stuff
Beside which I, the crafty victim, wait
Hours, while sleep sniffs and snarls its mild rebuff—
I wonder whether I can manage better
To pass time than by writing a verse-letter.

I'll probably manage worse; but there's one stanza
Anyhow; and another on the way
With help enough from lazy Sancho Panza,
Don Quixote may, somehow, get through the day.
Failing all else, that improvised cadenza
Lord Byron patented, wherewith to say
In bland digression everything that came
Into his head, may sit in on the game.

For my main trouble, as I can foresee
Already, is, and will be, even more,
That though I'd like this verse attempt to be
Expressive both of prophets and the law
(Maine's accent rhymes it) why, I lack the key
Even to unlock wit's and poetry's door.
Or briefly, though the impulse is O.K.,
I haven't, really, a damned thing to say.

The things most seriously on my mind—
Oh, war; free speech; my soul; atomic fission;
Whether the egg first saw the world behind
The chicken, or before; towards what perdition
Lapses all good and ill in humankind;
And other aspects moot to our condition—
Are much too hard to tackle at my best,
Far worse when all I'm trying to do is rest.

Then too, I've always felt that poetry,
Or even verse, if saying anything
(*Not* its essential business, but for me,
At present, easier anyhow than to sing),
Should say it tersely as the verb "to be,"

In language worthy of the kind of king
Kings seldom are, or ever were,—to say
Nothing of most who take their place today.

But there, you see, in spite of these convictions,
Already, now, with several stanzas done,
They are composed wholly of derelictions
From sense and duty; why, they aren't even fun.
But patience! If my personal prediction's
Halfway correct, your best bet is to shun
What follows even more sharply than what's past;
For heavy seas begin to hide the mast.

Well—to our muttons; which are jumping fences
Well out of earshot, if not out of sight.
This week, as you remember well, commences
My thirty-seventh year. I'm neither tight
Nor quite exactly sober. My defenses
Shaky and breached, yet hold. Eternal night
Enlarges to engulf my little world.
Soon, soon, my bugle bleats; my flag is furled.

All autumn long, through the magnificent slope
Of all the smoky year towards dissolution,
Much more than Nature—man's fate, and man's hope—
Have, in that avalanche, been in full collusion
Caught, shaped, and colored, even, on a scope
Grand as man's very being; a diminution
As huge to witness, and as full of grief,
As if each star were but a falling leaf.

1945

—

I walked into a wasted place,
And laid my head against a stone.
I heard its humming and the stars
Appear. I was alone.

I was alone and in such hope
(The cooling stone, the pointed stars)
I cried the name of God; proud tears
Sprang.   (The sharp stars.)

I challenged Him that he should send
The cruellest champion of his choice,
All ire, and raving wings, I prayed,
In my angry voice.

And sleeping, opened like a bride
To all the dream would surely bring.
And fought (or such as I recall)
My wounded King,

A city, and a wife and son,
Ten thousand masks of fear and law,
And faceless creatures of the depths:
And woke, in awe.

The stars were tired. The stone slept.
Colors hinted themselves. I knew.
The Angel had stood near, and gone.
Gently, the night turned blue.

1945

We soldiers of all nations who lie killed
Ask little: that you never, in our name,
Dare claim we died that men might be fulfilled.
The earth should vomit us, against that shame.

We died; is that enough? Many died well,
Of both sides; most of us died senselessly.
Ask soldiers who outlived us; they may tell
How many died to make men slaves, or free.

We died. None knew, few tried to guess, just why.
No one knows now, on either side the grave.
If you insist you know, by all means try,
That being your trade, to make the knowledge save.

But never use, not as your honor sorrow,
Our murdered days to garnish your tomorrow.

1945

November 1945

I

Now on the world and on my life as well,
Ancient in beauty, infant in such fear
As no time else had dreamed, nor shall dispel,
Loosen the ashes of another year.
Whether by nature's will, man's or my own,

I who by chance walked softly past a war
Shall not by any chance the world has known
Be here, and breathing, many autumns more.
Only, with all who in past worlds have died,
I had, till lately, faced my death secure,
Knowing my hunger only was denied;
All I most loved and honored would endure.
But this year, dying, struck wild as it fell,
Ending itself, me, and the world as well.

II

This being so, and thirty and five years
So nearly vanished, and so little used;
All delights turned as trivial as all tears,
All meanings altered and all hopes refused;
By what means shall I, in what little while
Abides my being, on such narrowed span
As will and world allow, find out that trial
Of strength wherethrough, well fought, I die a man?
O long, long, idle in tribulation,
Grown fat in all I did because I must,
I dreamed at least I knew my own salvation:
Now I begin to wake, and it is dust.
Where is the Angel in whose rage alone
Wrestling, I live? The night is nearly gone.

1945

Christmas 1945

Once more, as in the ancient morning,
The slow beasts, the fierce new-born cry;
And, in the heart the dreadful warning:
       Is it I?

All each heart holds of love, resolves
Once more, today, in angry grief,
Enduring courage; and dissolves
       In unbelief.

The Magi's gifts are subtle bribes:
The shepherds worship clock and wage:
In rattling arms, roared diatribes,
       Wakes the new Age.

And even now, at the town gate,
Welcomed by many, fought by few,
The clangor grows, of Herod's hate
       In the morning's blue.

And, in the straw, they hear; and stay.
All that is brave and innocent,
All that is love, reborn today,
       Is its time spent?

Where shall He flee, whose force is naught?
Where lies that Egypt which sufficed
Of old, now that each man is wrought
       Herod, and Christ?

1945

―――

How many little children sleep
To wake, like you, only to weep:
How many others play who will
Like you, and all men, weep and kill.

And many parents watch and say,
Where they weep, where they play,
"By all we love, by all we know,
It never shall befall them so."

But in each one the terror grows
By all he loves, by all he knows,
"Soon they must weep; soon they shall kill.
No one wills it, but all will."

But in each one the terror moves
By all he knows, by all he loves.
"Soon they will weep; soon they will kill.
No one wills it, but all will."

mid-1940s

Sonnets

Who was that boy, ranging the ruined hill,
Spine humbled to the horse's huge, light ghost,
Who would not lay the burden down until
He found the place he knew would please it most:

Then opened the rude ground and tenderly,
But without tears, buried the old, great frame,
Dressing the grave with leaves, that none might see;
And, standing straight, first saw the eyes of shame?

Oh it was I; no doubt but it was I;
Nor doubt, I fear, what ghost I put away:
But how I killed my carrier, and why,
I cannot fathom; far less could I say
Where one might seek, who cared to prove such things,
The lost, betrayed, mangled, magnificent wings.

———

I bore my bearer on a wasted mountain,
His weight being nothing, though the frame stayed
    whole
(But for the wings); yes, it was to that Fountain
Where first I saw him drink, I took his soul:
So cloyed with clay, so stiffened full of stone,
I hardly forced it open for his rest,
Where once a liquid more alive had grown
Than ever cherished in a mother's breast.

By what cause, right, or means, ever should I
Grieve? The immortal spring itself is dead.
Tearless I laid my killed soul to the dry
Root of his nurture. Yet the poor place bred
Just damp enough to lift up leaves in time
To mark the grave, heal the wound, and hide the crime.

—

O I begin to know: neither could live
Long, and the other gone; it lay with me
Once I had broken him, with me, to give
Earth, or refuse, his need. O now I see.
Only by flying could he know his thirst.
Only by drinking of her could he fly.
Only his absence filled her. But, wetnursed,
After a time, the aching breast goes dry.
And all that while I bent his mouth away,
It was not only he who slowly died.
The starving water shrank into the clay.
She became barren, who was once his bride.
And I, who parted them, for this return:
What then of me? in what hell shall I burn?

—

Just this: from now on, to go on foot,
Knowing what I have ridden, and deprived.
From now on, knowing what it is I put
To death, and what it is to have survived.
Wondering, while I can, if it be true
Water that broods here, or the spring's last tears:
And what, if anything, might be to do
To remedy the ruin of these years:
And knowing, knowing hopelessly, that I
May labor all I please and by God's grace
May break new water though the world be dry,

Yet never find a mount to take his place.
For by my blind will now my only one
Lies dead and buried here. From now on.

1947

A Lullaby

Sleep, child, lie quiet, let be:
Now like a still wind, a great tree,
Night upon this city moves
Like leaves, our hungers and our loves.
  Sleep, rest easy, while you may.
  Soon it is day.

And elsewhere likewise love is stirred;
Elsewhere the speechless song is heard:
Wherever children sleep or wake,
Souls are lifted, hearts break.
  Sleep, be careless while you can.
  Soon you are man.

And everywhere good men contrive
Good reasons not to be alive.
And even should they build their best
No man could bear tell you the rest.
  Sleep child, for your parents' sake.
  Soon you must wake.

1949

Lines Suggested by a Tennessee Song

1

Mary was the sweetest gal
a hundred mile around.
Lively and kind and good to see
as ever might be found.

The young men hung around her porch
till waylong in the night.
She never teased, nor give false hope.
She never let them fight.

A cousin come from down the cove
and marrying was his aim.
And when he left he took her love.
Joseph was his name.

Her pappy set the wedding day
when she would turn fifteen.
Joseph was aged three times her year,
but the best man ever you seen.

So Mary stayed the winter through
brushing her housework up.
And every Sunday regular
Joseph would show up.

And she grew prettier day by day
into a full young woman,
so sweet to see that Joseph felt
afeared, umble and common.

Why should they come such luck to me,
he'd wonder in his praying.
I'm old, and slow, and ornery—
God said, what's that you're saying?

You are the goodest man I know
in all this countryside.
Therefore I choosed you for this gift
of Mary for your bride.

Now listen quiet and hear me out:
You must not take her to your bed,
not for a time, nor pester her
over no maidenhead.

Mary is pure and true to you,
she'll live with you alone.
But her first borned, I warn you now,
He will not be your own.

Now you must care for Mary's health,
and Him, right from His birth.
The father of this little child
is nary man on earth.

And you must never think no thoughts
nor bother your kind head.
Mary will come in right due time
a virgin to your bed.

And him that you must call your son,
see you do right by him.
He is more lovely in my sight
than storms of seraphim.

And Joseph said: I hear you, Sir.
I caint quite understand.
But hold your orders in my heart
wrote out in your own hand.

God telled these mysteries to him
through angels in a dream.
Joseph waked up and watched around.
The dark was all agleam.

And like a match struck on a stove
it faded and was gone.
And Joseph laid awake and prayed
till the winder showed the dawn.

2

One clean march morning Mary was
a-training up her flowers
out of their buckets on the twine
in the dewy hours.

She heared the garden gate swing round.
She looked up and she seen
great wings of a white butterfly
that stood and called her Queen.

It warnt no butterfly on earth
she knowed, and knowed it well.
She seen, quick as her eyes could stand,
hit was Archangel Gabriel.

Mary, he says, God sent me here
to learn you what he aims to do.
He aims to send his son on earth.
The mother will be you.

Be not afeared. The morning dew
goes rougher on them baby leaves.
Right now the Glory works in you.
Right now your womb conceives.

Your boy will be the finest
that ever any mother bore.
Store up his childhood in your heart,
it must holp heal a heart that's tore

right to a rag one awful day
when you fall down before a cross
wishing mankind for ever damned,
counting up nothing but the loss.

God holp you then. And sure He will.
God keep you now. Your time is nigh.
Don't fear for Joseph, he's been told.
Now I must go. Good-bye.

And still as a fish in shiny branch
dodging the sunlight from his side,
Gabriel was there in all his light
and then warnt noplace hair nor hide.

3

They laid down in a cold black barn,
the stars worked through the walls.
The ox and the jackass kept them warm,
a-studying in their stalls.

The old hens grouched along their roost,
the Gobbler riffed his wing.
Out on the mountain niggers heared
the glorying angels sing.

And he come out and took his breath
peaceful as ary mouse.
And in the sky there opened up
a star over that house.

Bashful they come and kneeled them down
before that new borned child.
Good Joseph trimmed the lantern.
The gal laid easy and smiled.

She could a had the best hotel,
doctors, a fine gold ring,
name in the papers and winter flowers,
    For He was King.

He could a had the Mayor there,
a-waiting down the string
from the Governor and the President
    For He was King.

Ginseng root from Siler's Bald,
a star in the sky, a bird on the wing,
a kiver wove a ripe peach wool,
    For He was King.

He could a ordered Summer there,
Summer'd a skipped her Spring.
He could a never come to us.
    For He was King.

He did not need no company,
playpretties, nary a thing.
He come to us the manner he come.
    For He was King.

undated

Exiit Diluculo

Exiit diluculo
rustica puella
cum grege, cum baculo,
cum lana novella.

Sunt in grege parvulo
ovis et asella,
vitula cum vitulo,
caper et capella.

Conspexit in cespite
scolarem sedere:
quid tu facis, domine,
veni mecum ludere.

In the smallest light of day,
    Country Girl came walking;
Wool and spindle strung for play,
    All her young ones talking.

In her little herd she brought
    Lamb, and baby donkey,
Bull-calf, and the calf half-wrought,
    Kid, and the kid manqué.

Then found an Intellectual
    Waking in the pasture;
And said, "Can't we be sexual?
    Mister, at least I asked you."

c. 1949–50

Draft Lyrics for *Candide*

I *Culture Song*

Martin speaks enthusiastically of the Governor's paintings.

GOVERNOR (*speaking*)
    O really? I try not to look at them. I bought them out
    of vanity; Conspicuous Waste.

As he sings, he points out recognizable masterpieces; a
       landscape, a nude, a Madonna & Child.

GOVERNOR (*singing*)
Landscapes tire me, just to see;
   Nudes are so explicit.
The child on the Madonna's knee
   Is overweight (or is it?)
To walk through that would be a bore,
And this, one hardly could adore,
   And her, one cannot visit.

CANDIDE (*speaking*)
    Don't you admire Mythical Subjects?

GOVERNOR (*speaking or recitative*)
    They confuse me.
       (*or:*)
    They confuse evident subterfuge with sub-evident fact.

MARTIN (*speaking*)
Still-lifes?

GOVERNOR (*speaking or recit.*)
Intimate portraits of inedible food?

CANDIDE (*speaking*)
Ruins?

GOVERNOR (*speaking or recit.*)
I am a man of destiny; they depress me.

CANDIDE (*speaking*)
But if you can't paint such things, what *can* you paint?
What's painting *about*?

GOVERNOR (*speaking*)
About?

GOVERNOR (*singing*)
Why, even I might like the Mud-Pie Art,
If only it left out the Mind and Heart.
Only Pure Nothing, shot down on the wing,
Can hope to please One Who Has Everything.
If the Master, after full deliberation,
Would portray upon blank canvas What Is Not:
Whitest white on whitest white—, what
    pigmentation!—
One ultimate, ineffable Dot!

The dialogue leads to Books.

GOVERNOR (*speaking*)
O really?
I acquire them but I fear I can't admire them.
These solemn, interminable statements of the Old
Home Truths are a bit stale, for my taste.

GOVERNOR (*singing*)
War is Wasteful, writers say;
  Love is the Solution.
Misery Hurts. Pride Has His Day.
  Beauty's an Illusion.
War, Love, Beauty, Misery, Pride—
Pardon the impolite aside—
  Bore me to pollution.

CANDIDE (*speaking*)
Don't you like novels?

GOVERNOR (*speaking or recit.*)
Those dreary diagnoses of the Troubles of Mankind?
"I Was Hungry?" "Mummy Never Tucked Me In?"
  My mother *starved* me!

MARTIN (*speaking*)
Poetry?

GOVERNOR (*speaking or recit.*)
The words in a line of poetry are small, hunted,
intensely lascivious wild animals, huddling together
in a dark hole, and interbreeding like mad.

CANDIDE (*speaking*)
History? Biography?

GOVERNOR (*speaking or recit.*)
But all things human: be wholly alien.

CANDIDE (*speaking*)
But if you can't write about people, or the old, great truths, what *can* you write about?

GOVERNOR (*speaking*)
About?

GOVERNOR (*singing*)
Why, even I could love the Loudmouthed Art,
If only it left out the Mind and Heart.
Only the owner of the Signed Edition
Rightly consigns the Author to Perdition.
If the Writer, on new paper, after bleeding
Out his brains about the Time That's Out Of Joint,
Reduced all language to the ultra-special pleading
  Of the Period's ineffable Point!

The dialogue leads to Music.

MARTIN (*speaking*)
I like the early madrigals of Monteverdi.

CANDIDE (*speaking*)
I like a tune I can whistle.

GOVERNOR (*speaking*)
O really? I detest music; it makes my ears ache.

GOVERNOR (*singing*)
> Song itself is bad enough;
>> Singers gild the lily.
> Snarling, mooing, whinnying, gruff,
>> Uniformly silly.
> Violin, oboe, trumpet, gong,
> All the rest, are Bloated Song:
>> I loathe them, willy-nilly.

CANDIDE (*speaking*)
> Don't you like Opera?

GOVERNOR (*speaking or recit.*)
> Hyperthyroid anthropoids, screaming at each other in
> hysterical situations?

MARTIN (*speaking*)
> Masses?

GOVERNOR (*speaking or recit.*)
> The sung Mass is an ornately lubricious obfuscation
> of the celebration of a Sacrament which is beyond
> song or speech.

CANDIDE (*speaking*)
> The old, simple songs?

GOVERNOR (*speaking or recit.*)
> Like all music, even the simplest song seems to me an
> unconscionable waste of time: the longest possible
> distance between two points.

(*He perceives their puzzlement*)
   All music, after all, begins with this:—
(*He blows on a pitch pipe.*)

                                             —and,
   after evading and delaying the issue, it seems forever,
   triumphantly ends with this:—
(*He blows the same note.*)

CANDIDE (*speaking*)
   But—what's a man *supposed* to compose!

GOVERNOR (*speaking*)
   Supposed? Compose?

GOVERNOR (*singing*)
      Why, even I could like the Yowling Art,
      If only it left out the Mind and Heart.
      Only the man above such violence,
      Savors the beauty of Pure Siolence.

      If the Maestro, after lifelong meditation,
      Would purify pure purity with that
      One Tone which charms a man of cultivation:
         The ultimate, ineffable, F-Flat!

He sounds it on the virginal.

CANDIDE (*speaking*)
   He's the most educated man I ever met; he doesn't
   like *anything*.

II *Culture Song (Variant)*

O Really?

I deplore the earthy buttock and the heavenly breast
    Of the overexplanatory nude.
Landscapes tire me, myths confuse, Madonnas I detest.
    I loathe homely portraits of Food.

Yet even I might love the Dauber's Art
If only it eschewed the Mind and Heart.
On blank canvas, if the Master, after long deliberation
    On precisely how to epitomize What is Not,
Would impose on virgin white in virgin white—what
        pigmentation—
    The ineffable, inevitable Dot!

O Really?

War is Wrong, they inform us: Futile. Misery Hurts.
    And Love is Grand.
    Our Human Fate is Hard; but God is Love.
Beauty is Beautiful. Pride Shall Fall. I *think* I understand:
    And Literature, I've had my surfeit of.

Yet even I might love the Loudmouthed Art
If only it eschewed the Mind and Heart.

On new paper, if the Poet, as a Scientist uses Number,
    Placed the one exact, unarguable Word!

Not an orgiastic inkfest full of meanings which
     encumber;
   Just the Period's inevitable Surd!

O Really?

Bassoes grunt, tenors whinny, altoes moo, sopranoes
     snarl;
   And even if they didn't, there is Song.
The uterine strings, the bollicky brass, the woodwinds'
     swishy quarrel,
   Are Bloated Song, and equally long and wrong.

Yet even I might love the Yowling Art
If only it eschewed the Mind and Heart.

On pure silence, if the Maestro, after lifelong
     meditation,
   Killing every over-eloquent bleat and blat,
Would impinge the only note which charms a Man of
     Cultivation:
   The inaudible, ineffable F-Flat!

III *Pure Child (Sketch)*

CROWD
   Democratic Institutions
   Are the humble people's Voice.

FERNANDO

Democratic Institutions
Make me humble in your choice.

CROWD

Child, we charge you with the Future:
Make it shine, Pure Child, you must!

FERNANDO

I shall serve your Shining Future
As a sacred human Trust!

CROWD

Now that we have freely spoken,
Guardian, Leader, Master Mild,
Take our hearts' dear hopes in token:
Human Promise Undefiled.

On the foregoing 2 lines, dummy children are wheeled through the offering Crowd to stand, squadlike, at Fernando's feet.

FERNANDO
(*to Children*)
Follow me: we are Tomorrow.

In unison they lift palm-leaves in salute to him.

FERNANDO (*continuing*)
(*to Crowd*)
Sleep, dear friends, by dreams beguiled.

CROWD (*withdrawing*)
> Freed at last from Doubt and Sorrow
> Child, we bid good night; Good Child.

IV *Pure Child Song (Variant)*

CROWD

> (*Like middle-aged Sunday School children*)
>> Purest child, our hearts we leave thee,
>> All we hope and hold most dear;
>> Shining one, we must believe thee,
>> Fair one, fare where we would fear.
>>
>> We are old in Sin and Sorrow,
>> But our children cannot fail;
>> Build with them that Blest Tomorrow:
>> Poverty cannot assail.
>>
>> Heav'n on earth lies in your keeping,
>> All Man's Promise undefiled;
>> Guard our dreams while we lie sleeping:
>> *Child, good night; goodnight, good child.*

V *Pure Child Song (Variant)*

FERNANDO

> Soon, My People, I must leave you
> For the Final Human Quest:

CROWD

Purest Child, we must believe you:
All is surely for the best.

FERNANDO

Now that you have freely spoken,
I am humbled by your choice:

CROWD

Child, our children take in token
We are all a single voice.

FERNANDO
(to Children)

Follow me; we are Tomorrow:
(to Crowd)

Human Promise Undefiled:

CROWD

Child, redeem the race from Sorrow:
Child, good night; good night, Good child.

VI *Pure Child Song (Variant)*

(*Suggestion: he be called King Pure the First, not Third.*)

FERNANDO

My mother was a bulrush, my father was a mandrake
root.

CROWD

Bulrush! Mandrake root! Almost unheard of!

FERNANDO

Goodnight, my people.

CROWD

Goodnight, good child. Good child, good night.

FERNANDO

. . . a new life for all poor children.

CROWD

Bless him! The nino! The darling!

FERNANDO

. . . a life in which they can bloom and flower.

CROWD

You hear? The Angel!

FERNANDO

I shall lead a children's crusade . . .

CROWD

Ahh!

FERNANDO

. . . in search of your Eldorado . . .

CROWD

Ahhhh!

FERNANDO

. . . and my only prayer is that we do not perish
before we reach there.

CROWD

Ohh! Nnoo!

FERNANDO

We will set up a children's city . . .

CROWD MEN

Awww!

FERNANDO

A city of eternal innocence . . .

CROWD WOMEN

Ohhh!

FERNANDO

. . . and call it by your name.

WHOLE CROWD

Mmmmmmmmm!

WHOLE CROWD

(. . . *as Candide and Martin board ship with sheep;
brokenly, across drums:*)

Pure!
The Holy City!
Innocent!
The Poor!

Our Children!
Mandrake!
Bulrushes!
Pure!

CHORALE

(After each stanza, they withdraw. After the 4th stanza, they leave stage.)

Blest Child, the beaten countenance of the Race
Gains now, through Thee, a new victorious face.
All we have never been, could never be
    We trust to Thee.

We die. But in our children we prevail.
Lead them, Pure Child, where Guilt and Grief would fail.
Lead on, beyond despair, defeat, defense,
    Our Innocence.

Thou whom the Mandrake sired, most magic Son,
Thou whom the Bulrush bred, thou Godsent one,
Moses, our young, to Promise Undefiled,
    Lead on, Pure Child.

The oldest human mandate ends in Thee.
We are the Last Poor. Safe in Thy Hands we see,
Shining, immortal, even as we expire,
    Our Hearts' Desire.

(A little later, offstage, just before the ship collapses, they sing:)

Good Child, Good Night.

VII *The Marquise's Song*

THE MARQUISE (*speaking*)
Then I shall call you my Meadow Boy.

THE MARQUISE (*singing*)
Meadow Boy, L'Haute Monde is dirty:
    Court malicious, Boudoir, coarse.
A sensitive woman pushing thirty
    Wilts with ennui and remorse.
I'd give it all for just one quiet
Conversation with a horse.

CANDIDE (*speaking*)
Some horses are very nice.

MARQUISE (*singing*)
Gold and crystal, silks and satins
Pall, and in God's time shall pass.
I'd give all of them for Matins
    Mumbled with the Peasant Class;
All, and more than all, for one sweet
Romp with animals in the grass.

CANDIDE (*speaking*)
You love Nature?

MARQUISE (*singing*)
Nature, Boy, is Mother's Mania.
    Only Man can Peace alloy;
Cascades, crags and sweet Silvania
    Touch my soul with tranquil joy.

Most of all, I love the Meadow;
Come into my Meadow, Boy.

CANDIDE (*speaking*)
I certainly admire a pretty sunset.

MARQUISE (*singing*)
We shall leap and play like wild things;
    We shall lie too still for words.
We shall sing, and twitter mild things
    Obbligatoed by the birds.
We'll eat grass, quaff Nature's Nectar;
Toast our flanks among the herds.

CANDIDE (*speaking*)
Excuse me, but what I've been trying to say is, that I
am, have been, and always hope to be, in love with
Mademoiselle Cune——

MARQUISE (*singing*)
Animals are so intuit-
    -ive; nimble, in the Mating Act:
They shall teach us How To—

CANDIDE (*speaking*)
Excuse me, Ma'am; Mademoiselle Cu——

MARQUISE (*singing; lost in it*)
Chimpanzees, the scientists tell us,
    Make it in five seconds flat,

Smashing all mammalian records:
   Blessed are the pure in heart.
(*She fans herself and speaks, vaguely:*)
   I'm afraid I'm losing my sense of Rhyme.
(*gallantly*)
   Very well: a *fig* for artifice!
(*softly*)
   Touch my face.

(*Suggestion: a little later, instead of "my darling one," she says: "My bull calf!"*)

VIII *Love Poet*

Candide and Cunegonde encounter, by chance, just where and as they did in Act I, Scene I; and, as before, gaze at each other with quiet wonder. But where, before, we heard only the first two phrases of the song, through the orchestra, now they sing; and now they see each other with a different kind of wonder.

CANDIDE
   One lost morning
   Love awoke us;
   Told us children how
      Love was all
   A dream, a hope, a vow.

CUNEGONDE
   Now once more, love,
   Love has found us;

BOTH

> Vows, hopes, dreams, are lost:
> See, love; Love sees:
> Sane, strong, healing:
> Knows all, and gives all.

Candide proposes marriage. They speak their marriage vows, between lines of a reprise of the Love Duet, which is now set as a Chorale Prelude; and which is now sung by the other players who are onstage.

CHORALE PRELUDE

CHORUS

> Now Love shows us:
> All men might be:
> All men cannot be:
>   All our hope:
> In Love's plain light we see.

> See how Love takes
> Man's true measure:

> Man's true hope begins:
> Head to hold us:
> Heart to bring us:
> One, in Love's sane hand.

1949–50

BIOGRAPHICAL NOTE

INDEX OF TITLES
& FIRST LINES

BIOGRAPHICAL NOTE

James Rufus Agee was born on November 27, 1909, in Knoxville, Tennessee. His father was killed in an automobile accident in 1916. Agee attended Phillips Exeter Academy and Harvard. He became a staff writer at *Fortune* in 1932. The Yale Series of Younger Poets published *Permit Me Voyage* in 1934. A project on Alabama sharecroppers, done in collaboration with Walker Evans, was intended for *Fortune* but, rejected by the magazine, ultimately came out as the book *Let Us Now Praise Famous Men* (1941). Agee was married three times, to Via Saunders (1933-38), Alma Mailman (1938–41), and Mia Fritsch (from 1944). He contributed movie reviews regularly to *The Nation* and *Time*, 1942–48. The novella *The Morning Watch* appeared in 1951. Agee worked on many screenplays, including *The African Queen* (1954) and *The Night of the Hunter* (1955). He died of a heart attack in New York City in 1955. *A Death in the Family*, a novel on which he had been working for decades, was published in 1957 and won the Pulitzer Prize. His correspondence with Father James Harold Flye, a lifelong mentor with whom he had studied as an adolescent, was published as *Letters to Father Flye* (1962).

INDEX OF TITLES AND FIRST LINES

AMERICAN POETS PROJECT